Nonviolent Resistances in the Contemporary World

This volume studies nonviolent movements as instruments of change in contemporary global politics. It presents case studies of civilian-led nonviolent efforts in India, Poland, and Turkey and analyzes how they have enabled people's voices, influenced popular resistance cultures, and pushed for change across the world.

The book discusses complex sociopolitical scenarios that challenge democracy, patriotism, and the question of identity across the world. It examines how popular resistance movements have been received by the media, subverted governments across the world, and how they have contributed to the development of new "protest paradigms." The volume brings together leading experts who explore the significant wave of nonviolent mass movements in contemporary global affairs to understand how these discourses can be leveraged to study peace and conflict today. The authors involve extensive pedagogical discussions, new tools, and techniques to map emerging political discourses to identify and explain how contemporary peace-conflict research can study nonviolent resistance and facilitate the development of new narratives in the future.

An invaluable guide to understanding social movements, this book will be a must-read for scholars and researchers of politics, governance and public policy, gender, and human rights.

Nalanda Roy is an associate professor in the Department of Political Science and International Studies at Georgia Southern University, USA. She is also serving as a visiting scholar with the Center for Genocide and Human Rights, Rutgers University, USA. She is the associate editor of the *Journal of Asian Security and International Affairs*. She also serves as the board member for *International Studies Review*, Oxford University Press; *Perspectives on Global Development and Technology*; *Journal of the Royal Society for Asian Affairs*, Routledge: Taylor and Francis Group; and *South Asian Survey*. She published a book titled *Bitter Moments—The Story of Indonesian Fragmentation* in 2015. In 2016 she published a book titled *The South China Sea Disputes—Past, Present, and Future*. In 2020 she published a book titled *Exploring the Tripod: Immigration, Security, and Economy in the Post-9/11*. Her next book was published in 2021 titled *Navigating Uncertainty in the South China Sea Disputes: Interdisciplinary Perspectives*. She is also on the board of directors with the City of Savannah and works for the Greater Savannah International Alliance.

Nonviolent Resistances in the Contemporary World
Case Studies from India, Poland, and Turkey

Edited by Nalanda Roy

First published 2022
by Routledge
2 Park Square, Milton Park, Abingdon, Oxon OX14 4RN

and by Routledge
605 Third Avenue, New York, NY 10158

Routledge is an imprint of the Taylor & Francis Group, an informa business

© 2022 selection and editorial matter, Nalanda Roy; individual chapters, the contributors

The right of Nalanda Roy to be identified as the author of the editorial material, and of the authors for their individual chapters, has been asserted in accordance with sections 77 and 78 of the Copyright, Designs and Patents Act 1988.

All rights reserved. No part of this book may be reprinted or reproduced or utilised in any form or by any electronic, mechanical, or other means, now known or hereafter invented, including photocopying and recording, or in any information storage or retrieval system, without permission in writing from the publishers.

Trademark notice: Product or corporate names may be trademarks or registered trademarks, and are used only for identification and explanation without intent to infringe.

British Library Cataloguing-in-Publication Data
A catalogue record for this book is available from the British Library

Library of Congress Cataloging-in-Publication Data
A catalog record for this book has been requested

ISBN: 978-0-367-56611-1 (hbk)
ISBN: 978-0-367-62408-8 (pbk)
ISBN: 978-1-003-10931-0 (ebk)

DOI: 10.4324/9781003109310

Typeset in Times New Roman
by Apex CoVantage, LLC

Dedicated to the ace soccer player and my beloved father and guru, Late Mr. Bhabani Kumar Roy

Contents

List of figures viii
List of tables ix
List of contributors x
List of acknowledgments xii

1 **Introduction** 1
  NALANDA ROY

2 **Civil resistance and building peace within societies** 6
  GEORGINA CHAMI

3 **Polish nonviolent resistance against foreign occupation 1795–1918: a post-revisionist perspective** 30
  JACEK LUBECKI

4 **Kurdish identity, resistance, and agenda-setting in a time of renewed Turkish hostility: social media and the HDP** 60
  NED RINALDUCCI

5 **Exploring the culture of digital resistance in India: The *Nirbhaya* effect** 96
  NALANDA ROY & STEPHANIE MAE-PEDRON

6 **Conclusion: will civil resistance work?** 133
  NALANDA ROY

Index 137

Figures

2.1	Integration of positive and negative peace	17
4A.1	Distribution of human topics	94
4A.2	Distribution of human rights subtopics	94
4A.3	Distribution of human rights topics for top 5% of retweets	95
4A.4	Distribution of human rights subtopics for top 5% of retweets	95
5.1	Alternative news sources	99
5.2	Significance of online symbols	100
5.3	Most useful function of communication technology	102
5.4	Strengthen relationships of communication technology	102
5.5	Biggest hindrance of communication technology	103
5.6	Drawbacks of access to unlimited information	103
5.7	Most common rape myths	106
5.8	Causes of a skewed sex ratio	110
5.9	Addressing consequences (skewed sex ratio)	110
5.10	Ranking of reasons for unreported sex crimes	111
5.11	Registered rape cases, cases convicted, and persons convicted for rape in Delhi (2005–2016)	117
5.12	Registered rape cases by women in India (2005–2016)	118
5.13	Conviction rate for registered rape cases by women in India (2005–2016)	119
5.14	Ranking of sex crimes	120
5.15	Most significant outcome of the *Nirbhaya* case	121

Tables

4.1	From HEP to HDP	64
4A.1	Human rights topics frequency distribution	91
4A.2	Human rights subtopics frequency distribution	91
4A.3	Human rights topics norm variations	92
4A.4	Human rights subtopics norm variations	93
5.1	Distribution of population for men and women in India (2011)	108
5A.1	Gene Sharp's 198 methods of nonviolent action	128

Contributors

Georgina Chami joined the Institute of International Relations (IIR) in 2014 as a research fellow. Before taking up this post, she lectured at the undergraduate level in the International Relations Unit, Department of Behavioural Sciences. She was the former Coordinator of the Caribbean Child Rights Observatory Network (CCRON) established in 2014 to monitor and analyze the rights of children within the Caribbean region. She was the recipient of the Central America/Caribbean Fulbright Visiting Scholars Program in 2010 and pursued research at Nova Southeastern University, Florida. Presently, she is coordinator, diploma program in international relations; internship coordinator, IIR; and faculty advisor, Harvard National Model United Nations (HNMUN) and UWI STA Model UN Club.

Jacek Lubecki received his PhD in political science from the University of Denver Graduate School of International Studies in 2000 and has been a faculty member at Georgia Southern since 2012. He teaches and researches mostly in the fields of comparative politics and military security studies and has also taught courses on global political economy and in American political thought. Professor Lubecki's research has been published in journals such as *Europe-Asia Studies*, *East European Politics and Societies*, *The Polish Review*, and *The New Ukraine*. He has also published in the popular magazine *The Armchair General*.

Ned Rinalducci is an associate professor of sociology at Georgia Southern University. His work examines religious and ethnic political movements and cultural identity. He teaches courses on political sociology, media and society, political terrorism, the sociology of nationalism, and ethnic and cultural identity and conflict. Dr. Rinalducci holds a PhD in sociology from Georgia State University, an MS in social psychology from Mississippi State University, and a BS in sociology and psychology from Florida State University. He is the two-time former president of the Georgia Sociological Association.

Nalanda Roy is Associate Professor in the Department of Political Science and International Studies and coordinator of the Asian studies minor program at Georgia Southern University. She is also the Inclusive Excellence Fellow with the university. Dr. Roy also serves as a visiting scholar with the Center for Genocide and Human Rights, Rutgers University. Dr. Roy is the associate editor of the *Journal of Asian Security and International Affairs*. She also serves as the board member for *International Studies Review*, Oxford University Press; *Perspectives on Global Development and Technology*, Brill Publications; *Journal of the Royal Society for Asian Affairs*, Routledge; and *South Asian Survey*. Dr. Roy is the author of numerous journal articles and books, including *Bitter Moments—The Story of Indonesian Fragmentation* (2015), *The South China Sea Disputes—Past, Present, and Future and Immigration* (2016), *Exploring the Tripod: Immigration, Security, and Economy in the Post-9/11* (2020), and *Navigating Uncertainty in the South China Sea Disputes: An Interdisciplinary Perspective* (2021). She was on the board of directors with the City of Savannah and worked for the Greater Savannah International Alliance. Dr. Roy also worked as the vice chair and the chair of the Asian committee with the organization.

Stephanie Mae-Pedron was the former undergraduate research assistant and has completed a bachelor's degree in Political Science and international Studies and a master's degree in social Science from Georgia Southern University. Stephanie has also completed a minor in Asian Studies under my supervision during her undergraduate studies at Georgia Southern University.

Acknowledgments

It is my great pleasure to thank my husband and my daughter for their loving support and constant encouragement. I am also thankful to my graduate research assistant, Amber Brantley, for her editorial assistance with my book. Amber is pursuing a master of arts, with a focus in political science from Georgia Southern University. Sincere thanks as well to my graduate school mentor, Dr. Yale Ferguson, Rutgers University, for his continued interest in my work.

1 Introduction

Nalanda Roy

> *A society in which there was no possibility of murder would be a better one, but a society in which there was no possibility of civil disobedience would be much worse.*[1]
>
> —Leslie Green

1.1 Importance of civil resistance

During the 19th century, the "legal resistance" movement was initiated in Hungary under the Habsburg monarchy. At that time, Hungarians campaigned for more autonomy and national rights within Austria-Hungary, gaining limited success in 1867.

In the early 20th century, Mahatma Gandhi (1869–1948) brought civil resistance to wider attention, demonstrating that a new form of struggle is possible, one that has a degree of superiority over other forms. In fact, Gandhi's work demonstrates the efficacy of civil resistance in producing outcomes such as independence and democracy.

Today, there is a significant need for a systemic investigation of all possible methods of nonviolent action to identify effective strategies for resisting oppressive regimes. Civil resistance is a powerful tool people use to fight for their rights, achieve freedom, and, above all, get justice without the use of violence.[2] Nonviolent resistance is a civilian-based method used to wage conflict through social, psychological, economic, and political means without the threat or use of force. These methods include acts of omission, acts of commission, or a combination of both. This edited volume, *Nonviolent Resistances in the Contemporary World*, explores the issue of nonviolent civil resistance and explains how such campaigns are becoming a significant feature of international politics.

In *Why Civil Resistance Works*, Erica Chenoweth clearly explains that civil resistance campaigns usually attract greater numbers because there

DOI: 10.4324/9781003109310-1

is a much lower barrier to participation.[3] However, while civil resistance may work well against some adversaries, it has not always proven effective against tougher regimes. For example, the "Arab Spring" uprisings offer several examples of effective nonviolent actions in Egypt and Tunisia as well as failures in Libya or Syria, where the situation turned bloody. In order to create an effective, functioning democracy there are many factors to consider, and civil resistance may be only one.

This volume aims to promote knowledge of how popular resistance has subverted governments across the world and to expand on relevant studies in the field of resistance. Whether it is the Black Lives Matter protest, protests against climate change, protests in Hong Kong, protests for indigenous people's rights, the Me Too movement, #Justice for Sushant Singh Rajput in the Bollywood film industry, or the Stop AAPI Hate movement, all these efforts have received a great deal of media attention and contributed to the development of the "protest paradigm" across the world. By simply observing contemporary global affairs, it appears that we may be in the midst of a significant wave of nonviolent mass movements in world history.

By focusing attention on these issues, we hope to encourage scholars to expand the range of texts and genres they explore in search of nuanced ideas and debates. The proposed project involves extensive pedagogical discussions to facilitate the development of new narratives. This volume will identify and explain how researchers can incorporate contemporary forms of nonviolent resistance into their research, build on the study of civilian-led nonviolent efforts, and develop the connection between the study of conflict and the study of peace.

This volume brings together leading experts who present significant insights into this extremely important but sensitive topic: the "culture of resistance."

1.2 Organization

This collaborative, edited volume is a Routledge Focus book. It is organized around a few specific case studies from around the world. Based on our case studies, readers should clearly understand the important and necessary elements of successful nonviolent campaigns. The case studies are focused on India, Poland, and Turkey. They explore complex scenarios that challenge democracy, patriotism, and the question of identity across the world.

Chapter 2 critically examines how, over the last five decades, civil resistance has become quite commonplace as a tool for organizations and a method of deployment by civilians. The author explains that as civil resistance peaked in the early 2010s, it became increasingly apparent that nonviolent campaigns by unarmed civilian groups had become a significant feature in the global arena. However, there is limited research on how civilian groups can influence trajectories of violence and peace. Consequently, the author examines underlying forces of violence as well as civilian-led nonviolent efforts as a means of building the connection between the study of conflict and the study of peace. The chapter draws on the research of peace and conflict studies philosopher Johan Galtung to explain the latter. Finally, the chapter explains how the study and practice of civil resistance has become an avenue for challenging different forms of violence, laying the foundation for peace within societies.

Chapter 3 moves back in time and begins with a discussion of Polish nobility. When the early modern state of Polish nobility disappeared in 1795, it was put down violently by aggressive, militaristic neighbors which met with armed Polish nationalist resistance. Mesmerized by French and American revolutionary mass struggles, leaders like Tadeusz Kościuszko (1746–1817) believed that a truly popular war would deliver independence against the hollow might of empires. The notion that a truly popular war can overcome all obstacles has become a leitmotif of anti-imperial nationalisms and movements around the world, going through several permutations since the 18th century. However, it was not violent struggle that won independence for Poland, but nonviolent resistance, coupled with a measure of pragmatic collaboration with partitioning powers, especially during World War I. The chapter explains how bitter division, not unity, has been the hallmark of the Polish nationalist movement during the partitions period, and similar divisions have been very much in evidence in other movements of national liberation.

Chapter 3 demonstrates that, like all such struggles, the fight for Polish self-determination created its own critical and endless dilemmas regarding the respective virtues of armed resistance vs. unarmed resistance, resistance itself vs. collaboration with the "enemy." These debates have been faithfully reproduced in the discourses of other nations in similar circumstances. Indeed, it is stunning how many national movements face similar dilemmas, go through the same phases of struggle, ask the same questions, and engage in the same strategic debates, all while seemingly (if not blissfully) unaware that all this has occurred in other nations.

In a stylized form, these debates pit, on the one hand, "violent romantics" (those who celebrate violent resistance as preserving and advancing "the national spirit" regardless of its typically catastrophic effects on the substance of national life) against "nonviolent pragmatists" (those who see most "romantic" actions as unrelieved foolishness). Chapter 3 explains in detail how the "pragmatist" faction can be divided between "pragmatic collaborationists" and "nonviolent resisters." Similarly, "violent" strategists have their own strategic factions: insurrectionists, partisans of protracted popular war, pragmatic manipulators of geostrategy, and so on. Such divisions on tactics and strategy are often along factional and partisan lines, resulting in bitter and sometimes violently negotiated clashes within the nationalist movement (see: Fatah vs. Hamas in Palestine, Piłsudski vs. Dmowski in Poland).

This chapter also explores specifically nonviolent components of Polish national resistance from a comparative and critical perspective. The author studied 19th-, 20th-, and 21st-century national movements in a systematic way to gain policy insights into nonviolent national resistance, past and present. The author raises questions like: What role does nonviolent resistance play in national movements? What strategic and tactical dilemmas does the struggle typically pose? And finally, how can we derive broader lessons from the Polish experience of nonviolent resistance?

Chapter 4 discusses issues of Kurdish identity, resistance, and agenda setting through social media. The chapter explains how the Kurdish people have historically faced a wide range of outwardly hostile policies throughout the region and countries they inhabit. Focusing on Turkey, home to more Kurds than any other single country, the chapter discusses the history between the Turkish state and its Kurdish citizens. It is a history that has been defined by discrimination, cultural genocide, terrorism, and violence. This chapter explains how the current AKP government of Turkey came to power in the early 2000s with policies that seemed set on accommodating Kurdish rights, and how that was not to last. Recent years have seen tensions and hostilities renewed and violence cross national borders. This chapter explores how the primary Kurdish political party in Turkey (HDP), became more than just the voice of Kurdish rights in Turkey, while experiencing extreme governmental repression. The party has effectively used social media for purposes of pushing non-violent democratic inclusiveness, resistance, and agenda setting. A content analysis of HDP's Twitter communications looks at what issues the party prioritizes and what issues resonate as the organization uses the power of social media to resist Turkish state oppression.

Chapter 5 explains the ghastly 2012 Delhi gang rape incident that sparked unparalleled public outrage in India. Following the incident, protestors demanded that the government take action to ensure reliable public transport, improve security, and improve investigative and judiciary procedures surrounding cases of sexual assault. Importantly, the activities and protests were largely coordinated online, and this chapter examines how these new modes of communication affected resistance during and after the incident. In particular, the author examines whether the scale of the demonstrations managed to change public perception regarding the reporting of sex crimes.

The author has compiled data from annual crime statistics in India that show a spike in registered rape cases in the years following the incident. The chapter also explains how the extensive public discussions regarding the issue of rape, as well as other common sex crimes experienced by women, may have lessened the stigma associated with reporting. However, the author also explains how a growing backlog of pending rape cases and relatively steady conviction rates—despite an increase in reports since 2012—suggests a possible combination of issues related to inefficiencies within India's judiciary system, the perpetuation of rape myths, and even social perceptions regarding the status of women in society.

Finally, Chapter 6 summarizes the findings of the previous studies, suggests several avenues of future research that can prove fruitful for policymakers and academics, and attempts to answer our key question: Will civil resistance work?

Notes

1 L. Green, "Civil disobedience and academic freedom," *Osgoode Hall Law School of York University* 41, no. 2/3 (Summer/Fall 2003): 381–405.
2 G. Sharp (ed.), *Waging nonviolent struggle: 20th century practice and 21st century potential* (Boston: Porter Sargent, 2005), 41, 547.
3 E. Chenoweth and M. J. Stephan, *Why civil resistance works: The strategic logic of nonviolent conflict* (New York: Columbia University Press, 2012).

References

Chenoweth, E., & Stephan, M. J. (2012). *Why civil resistance works: The strategic logic of nonviolent conflict*. Columbia University Press.

Green, L. (2003). Civil disobedience and academic freedom. *Osgoode Hall Law Journal, 41*(2/3), 381–405.

Sharp, G. (Ed.). (2005). *Waging nonviolent struggle: 20th century practice and 21st century potential* (pp. 41, 547). Porter Sargent.

2 Civil resistance and building peace within societies

Georgina Chami

2.1 Introduction

With the onset of the new millennium, there is a growing difference in how states, groups, and individuals communicate with each other. From large-scale interstate conflicts to intrastate conflicts, there is growing and greater acceptance of, and obligation to, the approach of nonviolence. As wars continue in different parts of the world, more optimism and encouragement have been created by groups, individuals, and some state agencies that pursue peaceful approaches to the difficult challenges of preserving life and living in peace and unity.[1] Of course, nonviolence is not new, and throughout history there have been communities and leaders who have encouraged fellow citizens and governments to restrain from violent ideas and actions. But far too often, such calls have been disregarded and overridden by the powers supporting violent action.

Based on current trends, it seems likely and realistic that the critical spaces for the culture of nonviolence and peace may develop and replace the culture of violence and war. Philosophically, nonviolence seeks to nurture and promote relations and structures among all peoples and states that do not employ ideas and approaches associated with violence. For thousands of years, many civilizations and religions worldwide have endorsed nonviolence—for example, Hinduism and Buddhism. Throughout history, nonviolent action has been successfully employed in various conflicts—slave trade abolition, trade union and workers' rights establishment, enfranchisement of voters, national independence movements, the settlement of interstate strife, and so on.[2] Nonviolent resistance and conflict transformation show a common commitment to "social change and increased justice through peaceful means."[3]

Nonviolence was advocated by inspirational role models such as Mahatma Gandhi, Nelson Mandela, and Martin Luther King. A more holistic approach to nonviolence was also popularized by peace researcher, Johan

DOI: 10.4324/9781003109310-2

Galtung. His research speaks of structural violence that is evident at the social, economic, political, and cultural levels. Several reasons ushered the development of nonviolence through the decades: the Civil Rights Movement in the United States and the overthrowing of the shah during the 1978 insurrection in Iran.[4] The demise of communism in Eastern European countries exhibited systematic and organized nonviolent action, deeply inspired by the philosophies of Gandhi and King. Increasingly, nonviolent action has been recognized as a strategic approach by marginalized groups and individuals to address structural imbalance and to lobby for justice and equality.

The increasing trend toward using nonviolent action is attributable to growing peace and feminist movements, the global stance against nuclear arms, and the spread of civil defiance of military service. These processes displayed new methods, using no arms or violence, that spread quickly.[5] Within the last decade, other incidents such as the "color revolutions" in Southeast/Eastern Europe and Central Asia and the "Arab revolutions" were manifestations of civil resistance.[6] In both circumstances, huge street protests led to the resignation or defeat of leaders deemed to be dishonest or dictatorial. Other demonstrations in places like Hong Kong, Belarus, and Iran demonstrated people's efforts at enunciating discontentment with their governments.[7] In many instances, these demonstrations occurred because negotiation was impossible or impractical.

On the other hand, nonviolent action has facilitated a change in power imbalances to the degree that parties are pressured to negotiate on alike terms to resolve fundamental grievances. Thus, it is apparent in countries where nonviolent actions are pursued that these countries are more likely to enjoy democratic rule.[8] Nonviolent action tends to be comprehensive and diverse movements comprising a wide section of society. As such there is greater representation, legitimacy, transparency, and inclusiveness of people. According to Chenoweth and Stephan, participation in nonviolent resistance campaigns "encourages the development of democratic skills and fosters expectations of accountable governance."[9] Thus, nonviolent actions have become central in building peace and placing pressure on persons, groups, and systems.

Nonviolent actions can be very influential in altering systems in which small minorities benefit from an unfair status quo and lead to the demise of political regimes due to discontentment with their performance. For example, within recent years, the Black Lives Matter (BLM) movement, which is primarily peaceful, has attracted hundreds of thousands of people, who often show up to condemn police violence against Black people. The movement is focused specifically on racially disparate police practices but also more broadly on systemic racism as well as on problems faced by other marginalized groups.[10] Part of the rationale for the loss of the presidency by

Donald Trump is attributable to his complacency on critical issues such as the COVID-19 pandemic and BLM. Amid a countrywide uprising over systemic racism, President Trump did not acknowledge the underlying issues or the shared pain of the protestors. Even polls showed that a majority of voters disapproved of Trump's handling of the protests.[11] These demonstrations also had a political message—one shared by many other activists across the country: "Vote Donald Trump out."

In light of the above, this chapter seeks to address nonviolent action as a method for building peace within societies. The first part of the chapter will provide an overview of civil resistance, its tactics/strategies, and the factors accounting for the rise of civil resistance and its popularity. Using Galtung's theory of violence, it will be shown how social, political, and economic structures (i.e., structural violence), as well as religious and ideological structures, exist that support and reinforce structural violence. These structures have created unease, disharmony, and chaos within societies and have given rise to civil resistance movements. Simultaneously, this perspective allows for the reconsideration of nonviolent action that allows a range of tactics and tools not formerly dominant among peace activists. The chapter concludes with how nonviolent actions lay the foundations for peace.

2.2 What is civil resistance?

Civil resistance is also commonly referred to as "nonviolent action," "nonviolent resistance," or "nonviolent direct action."[12] It is a method of campaigning for social, political, and economic changes, and tactics include protest, demonstrations, strikes, and noncooperation. The rationale for these actions is to change power in a conflict without resorting to violence as well as to build power and realize political goals. However it is called, civil resistance has become the backbone of political action universally. The advantage of civil resistance is that it seeks to alter power by raising awareness and participation by applying social, economic, and political pressure. It is hoped that powerful groups will act responsibly by ensuring that the needs and interests of other groups in society are met. However, nonviolent action, while aiming to balance power and ensure equity for all, does not always lead to viable changes.

For the purposes of this chapter, civil resistance (nonviolent action) will be defined as a type of political action that relies on the use of nonviolent methods.[13] It promotes respect for universal human rights with the hope of building more fair and inclusive societies. It is seen as an integral component of dealing with different forms of violence and also an approach to achieving peace and justice. Civil resistance promotes the use of other approaches of conflict intervention such as negotiation, dialogue, problem solving, and restoring cooperative relationships (e.g., conciliation, cooperation, restorative justice). Often, nonviolent action seems more appropriate in the early transitional stage of dormant asymmetric conflicts for empowering oppressed and disenfranchised groups seeking constructively and efficiently to achieve justice, human rights, and democracy without resorting to violence.[14]

Often, regimes, governments, and non-state actors rely on the support and respect of ordinary people to govern. Civil resistance challenges a particular status quo and requires commitment, courage, and a readiness to take chances. It is a powerful tool that can be employed by people to advocate for equality, justice, and self-determination—without using violence. Nonviolent methods can challenge unjust institutions in ways that can enable a more just and peaceful society.[15] Gene Sharp identified 198 methods of social, economic, and political nonviolent action.[16] These methods were categorized into three classifications according to their strategic function: nonviolent protest and persuasion, 54 methods; noncooperation, 103 methods; and nonviolent intervention, 41 methods.

History shows that most successful nonviolent actions are more dependent on the capability and skills of ordinary people.[17] As defined by experts, the term "civil resistance" refers to civilian populations successfully employing nonviolent tactics such as protests, boycotts, and practical resistance actions to express their discontent at any form of oppression, discrimination, and unjust social relations existing within their societies.[18] The word "civil" in "civil resistance" refers to the people who employ nonviolent methods to pursue social change. The study and teachings of nonviolent struggle are key social factors in reducing violence and supporting and building peace in society. Actually, the concept of conflict management/resolution originally arose from peace movements and social justice activism.[19]

One of the main challenges in the study of civil resistance lies with its definition. Even words used synonymously with civil resistance such as "nonviolent action," "nonviolence," "nonviolent resistance," or "unarmed struggle" can have diverse meanings. Despite differences in local cultures and contexts, the terms "civil resistance," "nonviolent resistance," and "nonviolent action" are often used interchangeably. Even though the terminology differs across authors, there is a common meaning as signifying unarmed individuals using different methods against an opponent whose power is seen as superior. Most nonviolent actions employ strategies focused on increased participation and planning.[20] The inclusion of more participants in nonviolent movements allows for greater legitimacy, makes them more difficult to infiltrate and repress, and lays the groundwork for continuing participation. Planning encourages creativity, imagination, connectivity, and sustainability among participants.

Nonviolence can be divided into principled and pragmatic forms.[21] Principled nonviolence is undertaken for moral reasons and advocates for justice, fairness, and grassroots democracy. It promotes secular and religious ethical ideals. On the other hand, with pragmatic nonviolence, the intention is a method of struggle concerned with the results nonviolence can achieve.[22] It focuses on methods of nonviolent action. These include speeches, marches, boycotts and strikes, hunger strikes, and sit-ins. Some examples often related to nonviolence include the US Civil Rights movement, Gandhi's Indian Independence movement, the Solidarity movement in Poland, the Argentine and Chilean resistance to military dictatorship. These cases of nonviolent struggle and action can be categorized by geographical regions as well as by issue areas.[23]

During the 1950s and 1960s, there was a wave of nonviolent campaigns. These campaigns were a struggle for social justice for Black Americans to gain equal rights under the law in the United States. From 1970 onward, there was a decline in violent insurgencies and a rise in nonviolent uprisings.[24] In the late 1980s, there were Eastern European revolutions as well as a number of movements against US-backed right-wing military regimes in Latin America. The period 2010–2019 witnessed the greatest thrust toward civil resistance recorded since 1900. Nonviolent resistance is becoming more common.[25] While most scholars have concentrated on the remarkable reduction in violence over the past few decades, there is generally less discussion on the increase of civil resistance. In examining hundreds of movements over the last century, Chenoweth observed that nonviolent movements were twice as likely to realize their goals in comparison to violent campaigns. This was due to the recruitment of people from a broader demographic representation. It is therefore a powerful way of shaping world politics—in the long term.

In the early 2000s, nonviolent resistance became a growing trend and a very effective one. Nonviolent resistance displays the disapproval, hostility, and unease felt by people toward oppressive regimes and systems. Some examples of nonviolent resistance include the peaceful actions confronting Russia-backed regimes, like the one in Kyrgyzstan, the Georgian Rose Revolution, and the Bulldozer Revolution of Serbia. These peaceful actions demonstrated the strengthening of the idea of civil resistance, as it allowed activists to actively meet, engage, and learn from one another. The Arab Spring uprisings—particularly in Tunisia and Egypt—followed a similar trend, becoming quite expansive. Since 2013, the BLM movement has been organizing nonviolent action to defund police forces and invest in Black communities. But now, today's demonstrations are increasingly and noticeably interracial, consisting of African American, Asian American, Latin, and white faces, which suggests a new phase of opposition.

Civil resistance and building peace 11

There are different explanations and studies that account for the rise of civil resistance. It became evident to people globally that pursuing this option was a more appropriate and effective approach for producing change. Nonviolent resistance has become a popular choice for political action and seems to have replaced armed struggle.[26] The engagement with information technology tools has made it easier to learn of events that were previously unknown. Greater internet access allows more people to acquire more information online via newspaper websites and social media tools.[27] The internet has become a vital communication tool globally. It is beneficial for nonviolent resistance because individuals can communicate one-to-one more widely and with the capacity to transmit text, pictures, and voice.[28]

Also, it became obvious that a majority of society is increasingly focused on justice, fairness, and safeguarding human rights and is resorting less to violence. This shift may have created increased attention and importance toward civil resistance as a tool for promoting human rights. Furthermore, in the post–Cold War era, there has been an increase in nonviolent action simultaneously with an increasing number of international nongovernmental organizations (INGOs).[29] These organizations are solely committed to sharing information about, and sensitizing people to, nonviolent resistance and its importance. Some of the organizations include the Albert Einstein Institution, the International Center on Nonviolent Conflict, Nonviolence International, and the Center for Applied Nonviolent Action and Strategies. This development has been positive for the civil resistance movement.

Equally important, the erosion of democratic rights is increasingly evident across the world and has generated mass protests in some countries like Turkey, Poland, and the United States. Within recent times, many people in the United States have embraced the notion of civil resistance and have become actively engaged in these movements. Moreover, the legitimacy of many democratic institutions within the United States is now being questioned with respect to their effectiveness in managing racial tensions, public health insecurities, and rising inequalities. As nonviolent movements occur because of shared common interests and issues, there is greater awareness and, consequently, growing support for civil movements across regions. Through the internet, people can identify with peaceful protesters and lobbyists from other regions on different issues. This in turn exerts more pressure on systems and governments to alter their behavior.

These movements have sought to highlight and seek redress for direct, structural, and cultural violence. Traditionally, these movements emphasized violence commonly known as direct violence. Direct violence is started by an identifiable actor who threatens the well-being of another person or group. But, over the years, other forms of violence have been included on the agenda such as psychological violence (bullying), violence against animals, school shootings, police brutality, ethnic discrimination, and—to some degree—domestic violence. Different kinds of violence, particularly structural and cultural violence, exist in most societies. Only reducing violence at all levels can assist with building and sustaining peace. Developing expertise and knowledge on how violence originates and operates at all levels is crucial in building and sustaining peace.

2.3 Galtung's theory of structural and cultural violence

Up to this point, the discussion has sought to explain civil resistance, its methods and strategies, and its growing significance universally. Now it is important to describe the forms of violence that exist and underlie societal issues and have led to civil resistance movements. These movements have become a unique method in challenging forms of violence within societies, organizations, and structures. There are multiple forms of visible and invisible violence that are opposed by people globally and have come to be challenged. However, nonviolent resistance is problematizing the limited understanding of violence. Drawing from Galtung's research on violence will form the basis for clarifying and elucidating forms of violence and how these can be eradicated.

Johan Galtung's theory of violence is widely uncontested in peace studies and allows for a deeper understanding of how ingrained and institutionalized violence has become within societies. According to Galtung, violence is no longer narrowly defined as direct physical violence. Today, violence has broadened to include structural, cultural, and environmental violence. Critical to this notion of violence is the systemic violence caused by an unfair system and the cultural legitimization of violence against others and the environment. Thus, peace must be seen as a holistic approach at removing from a system all forms of violence. Moreover, the security of people—human security—has taken the forefront. Galtung's articulation of direct, structural, and cultural violence offers a broader, more cohesive, and more comprehensive framework that shows different types of violence.

Johan Galtung's conflict triangle works on the assumption that the best way to define peace is to define violence, its opposite. He explained the conflict triangle in his "Violence, Peace and Peace Research" in 1969, making known the ideas of personal and structural violence. In 1990, he introduced the concept of cultural violence.[30] For example, Galtung recognized poverty as a form of structural violence and media admiration and exaltation of violence as a form of cultural violence. Galtung also saw peace and violence as closely linked. He considered peace as negative (absence of direct violence) and positive (presence of social justice). If violence is eliminated, then peace can be achieved (negative as well as positive). An understanding of how violence originates and operates at all levels and how and why violence is used, therefore, is necessary to develop a theory of peace.

Structural violence is built into the social system and manifests itself in the uneven sharing of power and access to opportunities in the socioeconomic, political, and cultural spheres of society. The influence and successful institutionalization of structural violence lie in its ability to maintain unfair, oppressive conditions without creating direct or deadly effects. The patterns associated with structural violence include marginalized people resorting to direct violence to confront systems, organizations, and structures that repress them. Often, those who profit from an exploitative system continue using direct violence to maintain their status. Moreover, competition for resources increases the levels of direct violence between marginalized groups. If there are no serious and concerted efforts at changing these structures and systems, direct violence solidifies group identities and ignites scapegoating of allegedly inferior groups.[31]

On the other hand, cultural violence is defined, as "those aspects of culture, the symbolic sphere of our existence—exemplified by religion and ideology, language and art, empirical science and formal science, that can be used to justify or legitimize direct or structural violence."[32] Galtung stated that "the study of cultural violence highlights the way in which the act of direct violence and the fact of structural violence are legitimized and thus rendered acceptable in society."[33] What eventually happens is the validation of prevailing or prominent social norms, which seemingly make direct and structural violence normal, "right," or acceptable. For instance, the idea that Africans are primitive and intellectually inferior to Caucasians was advanced to justify the African slave trade. These dominant ideas became so entrenched in different cultures that they had become prevalent and inescapable and were reproduced unopposed for many years.

While structural violence affects specific organizational or social structures, violence in turn affects people—cultural violence. Cultural violence refers to the beliefs, customs, and systems of legitimation with the help of which direct or structural violence is made probable, acceptable, and is, indeed, legitimated. Over the years, Galtung's understanding of structural violence has become a central element for the global scholarly debate on peace and conflict. The primary reason is that it provides an understanding of the effects of conflict on people in developing countries and allows organizational and social structures to be examined. Thus, Galtung explains that structural violence is indirect, avoidable violence built into structures where there is unequal power and, consequently, unequal life chances.

Rising economic injustice and inequality have polarized communities. An otherwise peaceful population in different areas of the global arena accepts conflict, particularly where a larger part of the populace feels unjustly treated or deserted as a result of economic and social advancements. Consequently, political violence among people is generally viewed as a component of the struggle against inequality—whether for ethnic, national, or religious reasons. At the social level, peace becomes equated with individuals being able to have access to peace, freedom, and full participation in the process of governance.

By distinguishing the different types of violence, efforts at sustaining peace can be advanced. Generally, it was accepted that peace must be seen in relation to two types of violence: negative and positive peace. Negative peace is the absence of violence. In order to create negative peace, we must explore ways to lessen and remove violence. A good example in this regard would be a ceasefire, which is direct and immediate. On the other hand, positive peace ensures social justice and equality and the absence of structural or indirect violence within systems and societies. It is characterized by the presence of harmonious social relations and the "integration of human society."[34] In order to explain positive peace, it is vital to comprehend structural violence, which refers to social structures or institutions that prevent people from meeting their basic needs and accessing their basic human rights.

It is important to note that peace, whether negative or positive, does not mean the absence of *conflict*. Conflict itself is not a negative event, as it allows for a better understanding and knowledge on how positive change and transformation can occur. What becomes important is that conflict is handled nonviolently and constructively. Accordingly, Turay and English expressed this idea clearly by saying, "[C]onflict is a fact of life and a reality for all of us. How we deal with it is how we embody our understanding of peace and justice."[35] This involves ascertaining and addressing the basic causes and conditions that contribute to direct violence. In many countries, the effect of violence has considerably diminished efforts at advancing economic growth and reducing poverty. It has also caused deep psychological and physical trauma as well as reduced the standards of living within many societies.

As previously mentioned, Galtung advanced the concepts of three kinds of violence: personal, structural, and cultural. Examples of personal and structural aspects will be provided. For Galtung, a good example of direct violence would be the case of the Burmese military junta. It was suggested that the Burmese military junta was an extremely oppressive regime that exploited child soldiers. These child soldiers were often victims of torture, rape, and forced labor.[36] On the other hand, structural violence occurs indirectly in that "there may not be any person who directly harms another person in the structure."[37] As such, the violence is ingrained in the structure and presents itself as uneven power and thus unequal life opportunities. A good example is the presence of racial discrimination in America. There are social structures that have developed over time, which systematically disadvantage African American men and women who suffer from unequal life chances and that manifest as racism. According to Farmer, the "suffering is structured by historically given (and often economically driven) processes and forces that conspire—whether through routine, ritual, or, as is more commonly the case, the hard surfaces of life—to constrain agency."[38]

Structural violence is embedded within the structures of social, cultural, and economic institutions and seems more unforeseen and deceptive than visible and discernible physical violence. As such, people are denied important rights such as economic well-being; social, political, and sexual equality; and a sense of personal fulfillment and self-worth.[39] Structural violence is an unfair framework that functions through powerful organizations and institutions that guarantee privilege among its leaders, prioritizing their political agenda and enforcing their approaches and ideas. The power imbalances indirectly result in injury toward others through exclusion and exploitation. Other examples of structural violence include homicides, suicides, war, gender imbalances, and racial disparities. Conceptualizing structural violence can help guide peace research by considering the conditions that are positively conducive to peace.

The study of cultural violence emphasizes the ways by which direct and structural violence are legitimized and thus become acceptable and commonplace in society. Cultural violence may exert itself even in contexts in which human and civil rights are legally in place. The slave trade was an example of cultural violence. Africans were enslaved, forced to work against their will, and were killed or died in the process—in Africa, on board ships, or in the Americas.[40] Over the years, cultural violence has become quite extensive, with whites seen as superior and Blacks as inferior. This has created considerable prejudices and unfair actions universally.

According to Galtung, the dominance of Western political structures has further weakened state structures in weak, peripheral states, which have caused internal problems for their people and cultures. There has been an increase in insecurities at the societal level that affect patterns of communal identity and culture. Further, at the beginning of the 21st century, because of the falling standards of living in some states, there was an increase in migration to developed states. Furthermore, fallout from intrastate conflicts and the clash of rival civilizational identities have led to refugee and internally displaced people crises. The absence of social justice in relation to the individual is seen as a significant aspect of building peace.

From the discussion, understanding how the international system has evolved and is presently structured will complement our understanding and explanation of the variables of contemporary peace. Reference is made to Galtung's structural violence approach in order to accomplish the latter.

Galtung discussed "positive peace," or a state of "social justice," realized in the absence of structural violence; this is opposite to "negative peace," defined as the absence of war. Moreover, "peace" is no longer an exclusive activity of the sovereign state. Peace has been reconceptualized and is seen as part of improving the governance of states; providing higher standards of living; and incorporating local civil society.

In spite of the need for communication between studies of peace and studies of conflict, there has long been concern that exchange is rare, in practice.[41] For that reason, the study of peace has been basically associated with how we understand violence. Essentially, little research has explored the evolution of the concept of nonviolence as a method in building peace in the international context. It is argued that nonviolence is more effective than violence. The upsurge of nonviolent movements globally has become a major feature of the 21st century. These movements challenge opponents on areas of unaccountable governance, systemic corruption, institutionalized discrimination, and environmental degradation. Civil resistance is an avenue to be explored in relation to building peace.

2.4 Nonviolence as an opposite to violence

Over the years, the concept of violence has developed and broadened considerably. Galtung's articulation of direct, structural, and cultural violence offers a unified framework within which all violence can be seen and explained.[42] In summary, he defines direct violence as harming other persons with intention, structural violence as "harm to humans as a result of injustices in our societies," and later he added the term "cultural violence." Cultural violence is the cultural justification of direct and structural violence. Each of them has their antithesis in the context of nonviolence. Different approaches to building peace and nonviolence respond to the different types of violence.

Galtung acknowledged that the terms "peace" and "violence" are linked to each other such that "peace" can be regarded as the "absence of violence."[43] For him, violence could be separated into direct violence (its visible aspect) and structural and cultural violence (its invisible aspects). According to Galtung, positive peace is the absence of structural violence or the presence of social justice. Contrary to negative peace, positive peace is not simply getting rid of something, but includes the idea of establishing something that is missing. Therefore, while getting rid of structural violence or social injustice, positive peace or social justice must also be created in its place. Galtung integrates negative and positive peace in Figure 2.1.

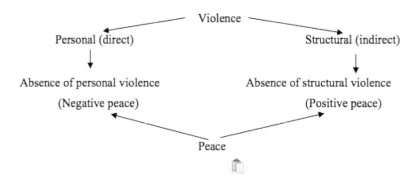

Figure 2.1 Integration of positive and negative peace
Source: Galtung, J. (1969). Violence, peace, and peace research. *Journal of Peace Research*, 6(3), 183. https://doi.org/10.1177/002234336900600301.

Direct nonviolence is the practice of employing nonviolent methods aimed at influencing conflicts without resorting to violence. Practical nonviolent methods and strategies are used to directly confront decisions, choices, laws, and organizations that treat humans unfairly. Struggles for the abolition of slavery, decolonization, elimination of patriarchal/male-dominated structures, and resolution of conflicts and imperialistic policies are all in keeping with the philosophy of direct nonviolence. People have also employed direct nonviolent methods against unlawful power holders and in confrontations with armed police and military forces for many years; many of them with successful results. Nonviolent tactics include marches, protests, vigils, civil disobedience, boycotts and sanctions, to name a few.

The motivation behind nonviolent action emerged from antagonistic relations between nonviolent challengers and the groups they targeted. The impetus for nonviolent action and struggle lies in the disruptiveness and the uncertain cause of action. According to Sharp, the methods of nonviolent struggle, noncooperation, and nonviolent intervention are formidable and result driven in peacebuilding. Sharp defines nonviolent action as "a technique of socio-political action for applying power in a conflict without the use of violence."[44] Some methods of noncooperation in nonviolent struggle include boycotting, suspending assistance and cooperation, and different forms of civil disobedience such as strikes and so on, while the nonviolent intervention method disrupts social and political activities and includes hunger strikes, protests, and sit-ins. His work outlines 198 different methods and shows nonviolent action is an effective method of achieving political change.[45]

Traditionally, the literature on civil resistance has focused on conflicts relating to open dictatorship and direct violence where political democracy is the goal of the challengers. In these situations, the focus is on freedom from foreign occupation, removing authoritarian regimes, preventing coups d'état, and eliminating visible discrimination. There is a sharp distinction between oppressor and oppressed and the subjects and objects of violence, which is easily recognizable. Galtung asserted that civil resistance might also be used to combat structural violence—that is, diffuse or systemic injustices and inequalities embedded in institutions or social relations that prevent people from meeting their basic human needs.[46] What are required are better regulated market relations; more equitable access to, and sustainable use and distribution of, resources; and transparent and effective governance structures.

On the other hand, structural nonviolence consists of systems and methods in place within societies that uphold cooperation, compromise, openness, fairness, and peaceful actions. A critical component would be the advancement of democratic institutions and systems that promote consensus building, inclusiveness, and accountability. And these are all elements in many traditional communities. Ensuring structures that promote these attributes will be central, to a large degree, to the fulfillment of political, social, economic, and cultural goals and rights. In situations of imbalanced access to resources and infringement of rights, a nonviolent structure allows people the prospect of addressing such conflicts through peaceful efforts. In such situations, "peaceful" combines tools of direct nonviolence as well as mediation, conflict transformation, and reconciliation.

Cultural nonviolence includes those aspects of our culture that promote nonviolent behavior, values, and qualities often seen in most cultures, religions, and beliefs. Even in times of volatility and violence, there have been individuals and groups who have used nonviolent techniques. Throughout history, people such as Mahatma Gandhi, Nelson Mandela, and Martin Luther King have used nonviolent techniques and made great sacrifices in the name of peace. Their philosophies continue to inspire people and movements in modern times that are opposing different forms of violence. This area of research may have been overlooked, as it is not seen to be as important as conflicts in which violence occurs. Yet peaceful actions are gaining recognition as vital examples of how to handle conflicts nonviolently. The need to document nonviolent movements and actions as an avenue for building peace cannot be underestimated.

2.5 Setting the stage for peace processes through nonviolence

The discussion on supporting and building peace is based on negative and positive peace understandings.[47] Negative peace is the absence of violence, and positive peace seeks to understand and address the root causes of conflict or violence. Within the literature, there are different weightings given to understandings of building peace as primarily concerned with negative peace or with positive peace. Some argue that it is looking at what the locals want: how the locals want to redesign the institutions that they will build coming out of periods of conflict. This gave rise to the concern with what are often called bottom-up approaches.[48]

Building and supporting peace does not mean eradicating violence. The challenge for building peace is how types of violence can be communicated and managed. Different methods can be employed in the interest of sustaining peace. Nonviolent action promotes social norms that avoid violence, helps to build trust among individuals and groups, and diffuses power throughout society. This allows for the empowering of groups who might otherwise be excluded, widening democratic participation, and appreciating intergroup communication. Nonviolent approaches can build peaceful communities.

Culture-of-peace debates have always centered their discussions on two approaches: building peace from below and above. Building peace from the top is where international institutions or regional actors are involved to a large extent. On the other hand, building peace from below gives primacy to local actors and the participation of affected communities in building peace.[49] Both approaches emerge from the literature about cultures of peace. As such, identifying and addressing conflict drivers is not the only important factor but also ascertaining and supporting the political and social dimensions that sustain peace. In this regard, sustaining peace is a shared task and responsibility that should be fulfilled by the government and all other national and local stakeholders, including civil society.

Advocates of nonviolence protest and lobby for institutions that are receptive to their needs and interests and advance social justice. Such institutions will have greater legitimacy and subsequently will act with greater authority. These institutions must gain the respect of people in order to be seen as legitimate and foster good relations between community members. Efforts at promoting peace within communities rely on action among community members that builds trust and thereby social norms favorable to negotiation, tolerance, and mutual respect. The features associated with nonviolent methods of engaging in conflict can contribute to building trust, cooperation, and confidence. Nonviolent struggle can also change the structural distribution of power in a community in ways that help build and sustain a culture of peace. There is greater need for cooperation and dialogue between those in authority and the local population to work collaboratively on sustaining peace within societies.

Nonviolent action has been especially effective in laying the foundation for peace processes and challenging disparities within societies. While such actions and movements may fully aim to protect civilians from violence, these movements are typically low profile. They can also have significant impact during periods of extreme violence, by highlighting the challenges faced by locals, and facilitate peace discussions, assisting in the upholding and preservation of the social structures that will consequently enable social recovery during the later stages of the peacebuilding process. Once a mass movement arises and unsettles the status quo, most regimes confront unarmed protestors with brute force, only to see even larger numbers of demonstrators turn out to protest the brutality.[50] It is evident that the rise of organized local nonviolent movements has resulted in a major drop in civilian casualties.

Nonviolent movements may also act as powerful sources of pressure for peace by uniformly pressuring opposing parties to come to the negotiating table.[51] These movements are expressions of dissatisfaction with conflictual situations and prepare the way for making peace. For example, the Women of Liberia Mass Action for Peace movement highlighted the increasing violence toward women during the Liberian Civil War. Public demonstrations, interreligious dialogue, and a national "sex strike" were organized to pressure both Liberian president, Charles Taylor, and Liberian rebel groups to participate in peace discussions. Even though the Women of Liberia Mass Action for Peace was not formally involved in peace negotiations, they played an effective and positive role. Their pressure was a key factor in encouraging the warring factions to participate in peace talks and finally reach a settlement.

Problems leading to nonviolent movements are generally believed to be multilayered, spanning social, economic, cultural, and political spheres. Problems to be addressed in this area may include security sector reform, producing or restructuring governance institutions, developing the means to allow the struggle for power to continue through peaceful channels, and instituting and monitoring elections. Democracy, good governance, rule of law, and human rights have become central to initiatives, processes, and activities geared toward peacebuilding. The notion is that democracies facilitate nonviolent governance and management of societal conflicts. However, the nature of democracy and the manner in which it operates remain debatable.

It is also important to focus on cultures of peace, social cohesion, and reconciliation. This can be done either through peace education or nonviolent dispute resolution systems based on the customary principles and customs of local communities. As such, it is critical to identify and emphasize strategies and actions that promote communication, negotiation, dialogue, and mutual respect among opposing parties. This would reduce and eliminate biases, stereotypes, and negative perceptions among different groups or communities and initiate trauma healing, reconciliation activities, and rituals that allow for recognition and awareness of wrongdoing by perpetrators. These activities are geared toward promoting emotional and psychological healing, social cohesion, and coexistence.

The ingenuity of nonviolence lies in preventing domination by breaking the cycle of violence. Nonviolent action aims at producing a balance of power that forces opposing sides to engage in dialogue, negotiate, and resolve their problems. Nonviolence offers people another avenue of resolving conflict without using violence. Nonviolent techniques are available to all and help break the cycle of violence and counterviolence in society. Interestingly, nonviolent action allows conflicts to be exposed and thus eliminates injustices being committed. Nonviolence is a way of humanizing human society.

2.6 Conclusion

Civil resistance (also called "nonviolent action," "nonviolent struggle," "nonviolent conflict," and "people power") is a practice for opposing political, economic, and/or social inequalities without using threats or physical violence. The most enduring definition for civil resistance comes from the work of Gene Sharp. By this definition, civil resistance is a technique of struggle employing methods outside traditional institutional channels for making change in a society. There are a wide range of tactics employed, including marches; demonstrations; strikes; various forms of noncooperation; and constructive actions, such as building parallel social, economic, cultural, or political institutions as alternatives to the existing repressive structures.

As of the mid-2010s, it has been documented and recorded that civil resistance is on the rise. Civil resistance is most effective when practiced communally, methodically, and strategically. As such, many scholars focus primarily on the use of civil resistance by popular campaigns and movements of people in a society. There are a number of factors that can account for its rise. These include a greater preference for peaceful movements; increased information and communication technologies; and greater emphasis on justice, fairness, and safeguarding human rights. Campaigns have intensified because of mounting inequities within societies and countries and the need to address them.

In a larger sense, peacebuilding involves a transformation toward more manageable, peaceful relationships and governance structures—the long-term process of addressing root causes and effects, reconciling differences, normalizing relations, and building institutions that can manage conflict without resorting to violence. Initiatives for building peace should fix the principal problems that trigger the conflict and change in the patterns of interaction of the involved parties. The main purpose of peacebuilding is to create positive peace, a social balance in which the surfacing of new disputes does not escalate into violence and war. Sustainable peace is characterized by the absence of direct, cultural, and structural violence. The main aim is to move people from a condition of extreme vulnerability and dependency to one of self-sufficiency and well-being.

Building and supporting peace have become associated with how violence can be managed and peace can be sustained. Galtung's structural violence theory provides an understanding of how peace has evolved in the current global system and the variables that constitute it presently. Galtung's research showed how the global system evolved and produced the highly hierarchical, uneven, and asymmetrical system, which has produced economic, social, and political consequences for the individual. Given the prevalence of intrastate conflicts, Galtung argued that a more holistic approach to maintaining peace beyond just military and security priorities needed to be taken. This approach would deal with domestic issues such as democratic legitimacy, economic equity, and governance within countries and increase chances of justice, equality, and transparency among the citizenry. Clearly, a multidimensional approach for peace is required.

Galtung also discussed the structural relations of dominance existent in the political, economic, military, cultural, and communication dimensions. The entire structure of dominance has to be understood. In line with the "center-periphery" analysis, Galtung argued that one must look inside societies to understand the effects of interactions among them. Therefore, in order to understand the effects of the level of disharmony and discord within, the direct and indirect causes (root causes) must be understood. Not only does structure enhance or diminish the stimulus for conflict, but also the culture in which the conflict occurs.

Once these root causes are assessed, then the peace researcher is able to identify those measures that can facilitate or enhance peace initiatives. Furthermore, attempts to sustain positive peace via short- to medium-term intervention are unachievable. The shift from state security to human security has allowed for a wider notion of peace to be developed. Consequently, the protection and welfare of the individual citizen or human being are central. Galtung's structural violence theory accounted for this broader notion of peace. The inclusion of civil society in addressing conflict is their capability to instigate change in their societies. Civil society plays a critical role in highlighting the underlying causes that need to be addressed if a sustainable and just peace is to emerge. Moreover, civil society can also sensitize the populace to the drawbacks of continued conflict and provide ways of brokering peace through constructive engagement.

Ideally, for forms of violence to be addressed, it becomes imperative to devise peace strategies for the global system. As such, there are three levels in which strategies can be recommended: the individual, the societal, and international levels. At the *individual level*, the focus is on improving education. Educating people is critical to building peace, as it allows people to gain knowledge and insight on policies, issues, and challenges being experienced. Local capacity building is also a critical component to any efforts associated with building peace. The aim is to ensure that there is an effective and capable local capacity to support nonviolent actions aimed at building peace.

In terms of the *societal level*, the benefits of democratization as an effective peace strategy in conflictual societies are undisputed. From many peace and conflict research reports, it has been proven that democracies are less likely to go to war *between themselves*. The rationale is that democracies tend to seek peaceful means of settling conflict. But for this factor to be beneficial to the society, the inclusion and input of the local population remain fundamental. Local civil society comprises the best people to devise what is in their best interest. Another important area for sustaining peace at the societal and international levels is to increase prosperity. Poverty and the uneven distribution of wealth are deep-seated root causes of war. Another important factor in increasing prosperity is free trade. Moreover, those economic relationships and arrangements contribute to a more sustained peace.

Critical to the above is the international system. The structure of the international system is characterized as an uneven one in terms of the socioeconomics between countries. This disparity has widened over the years and is directly associated with peace and violence. The aim of peace strategies, therefore, is to limit the insecurities that result from it. It is essential that strategies are devised to assist societies recovering from conflict to develop the necessary local capacity and institutional infrastructures in order to decrease the insecurities. Furthermore, rehabilitation and reconstruction projects through the Bretton Woods Institutions must be more flexible and sensitive to the conditions of the local environment.

Undoubtedly, peace has moved into socioeconomic spheres of the international society. There can be no social or political stability where there is discrimination; widespread poverty; or vast differences in income, equality, and economic opportunities. Thus, peace entails the fostering of cooperation among human groups with ostensibly different cultural patterns so that social justice can be achieved. In addition, human potential will freely develop within democratic political structures. Therefore, peace is defined as "the absence of violence and fostering of conditions for increasing political freedom and social justice in which conflicts could be resolved by nonviolent means."

In light of this, nonviolent actions are critical, and their inclusion in peace processes should be promoted/advanced. These actions involve the participation and support of the local population. As such, they can influence popular buy-in for peace discussions, highlight key challenges affecting the general population, and place pressure within societies to effectuate change. Of course, nonviolent action is not a cure for violence, but present-day trends suggest an increasingly significant role to be played by these movements in sustaining peace. The surge in nonviolent action is due to its growing significance, effectiveness, and potential to influence change. This is evident with the huge numbers of people participating in nonviolent movements for change in places like Hong Kong, Indonesia, Chile, and Russia.

It must be acknowledged that while nonviolent action is a rising phenomenon, it will most likely face severe opposition and thus become violent. Despite this, civil resistance continues to grow and strengthen universally. Protestors are searching for alternative methods of instigating and evoking constructive change. This in no way suggests that people have lost hope on institutional means of change. Instead, it signifies that another method such as civil resistance is being employed in an attempt to get institutional means to work again. From time to time, civil resistance is needed to revitalize democratic processes. As more and more people are opting for nonviolent actions to address their grievances, then closing the gap between nonviolent action and peacemaking becomes imperative and critical.

Notes

1 V. Floresca-Cawagas and T. Swee-Hin, "Institutionalization of nonviolence," in L. Kurtz (ed.), *Encyclopaedia of Violence, Peace and Conflict* (Newyork: Elsevier Inc., 2008), 1013–1025.
2 L. J. Cohen and A. Arato, *Civil society and political theory* (Cambridge: MIT Press, 1992).
3 J. P. Lederach, *Preparing for peace: Conflict transformation across culture* (Syracuse, NY: Syracuse University Press, 1995), 15.
4 K. Schock, *Unarmed insurrections: People power movements in non-democracies* (Minneapolis: University of Minnesota Press, 2005).
5 M. Martinez Lopez, *Ni paz, ni guerra, sino todo lo contrario: Ensayos sobre defensa y resistencia civil* (Granada: Educatori, 2012), 28.

6 V. Dudouet, *Powering to peace: Integrated civil resistance and peacebuilding strategies* (Washington, DC: International Center on Nonviolent Conflict Special Report Series No. 1, April 2017), 11.
7 Y. Serhan, "What Belarus learned from the rest of the world," *The Atlantic*, August 26, 2020, https://www.theatlantic.com/international/archive/2020/08/belaurus-protest-tactics-hong-kong/615454/.
8 Erica Chenoweth and Maria J. Stephan, *Why civil resistance works: The strategic logic of nonviolent conflict* (New York: Columbia University Press, 2011); Adrian Karatnycky and Peter Ackerman, *How freedom is won: From civic resistance to durable democracy* (New York: Freedom House, 2005).
9 Chenoweth and Stephan, *Why civil resistance works*, 207.
10 J. Cobbina, *Hands up, don't shoot: Why the protests in Ferguson and Baltimore matter, and how they changed America* (New York: New York University Press, 2019).
11 B. Bennett and T. Berenson, "How Donald Trump lost the election," *Time*, November 7, 2020, https://time.com/5907973/donald-trump-loses-2020-election.
12 Maia Juan Masullo Hallward and Cécile Mouly, "Civil resistance in armed conflict: Leveraging nonviolent action to navigate war, oppose violence and confront oppression," *Journal of Peacebuilding & Development* 12, no. 3 (2017): 1–9, https://doi.org/10.1080/15423166.2017.1376431.
13 A. Roberts and T. G. Ash, *Civil resistance & power politics: The experience of non-violent action from Gandhi to the present* (Oxford, UK: Oxford University Press, 2009).
14 V. Dudouet, "Nonviolent resistance and conflict transformation in power asymmetries," in M. Fischer and B. Schmetzle (eds.), *Berghof handbook for conflict transformation* (Berlin: Berghof Research Center for Constructive Conflict Management, 2008).
15 M. Bartkowski, "Do civil resistance movements advance democratization?" *ICNC Minds of the Movement*, September 27, 2017, https://www.nonviolent-conflict.org/blog_post/civil-resistance-movements-advance-democratization/.
16 G. Sharp, *The politics of nonviolent action. Part two: The methods of nonviolent action* (Boston: Porter Sargent Publishers, 1973).
17 Chenoweth and Stephan, *Why civil resistance works*.
18 M. Randle, *Civil resistance* (London: Fontana Press, 1994); Peter Ackerman and Jack DuVall, *A force more powerful: A century of nonviolent conflict* (New York: St. Martin's Press, 2000); Chenoweth and Stephan, *Why civil resistance works*; Roberts and Ash, *Civil resistance & power politics*; Schock, *Unarmed insurrections*.
19 E. F. Dukes, "Structural forces in conflict and conflict resolution in democratic society," in H. W. Jeong (ed.), *Conflict resolution: Dynamics, process and structure* (Aldershot: Ashgate Publishing, 1999), 155–171.
20 M. E. King, "Nonviolent struggle in Africa: Essentials of knowledge and teaching," *Africa Peace and Conflict Journal* 1, no. 1 (2008): 19–44.
21 B. Martin, "Technology, violence and peace," in L. Kurtz (ed.), *Encyclopedia of violence, peace, & conflict* (Oxford, UK: Elsevier Science & Technology, 2nd ed., 2008), 2045–2055.
22 Sharp, *The politics of nonviolent action*.
23 A. Carter, H. Clark and M. Randle, *People power and protest since 1945: A bibliography of nonviolent action* (London: Housmans Bookshop, 2006); A. Carter, H. Clark, and M. Randle, *A guide to civil resistance: A bibliography of people*

power and nonviolent protest: Volume one (London: Green Print, 2013); R. M. McCarthy and G. Sharp, *Nonviolent action: A research guide* (New York: Garland Press, 1997.)
24 E. Chenoweth and M. J. Stephan, "Future of nonviolent resistance," *Journal of Democracy* 3, no. 3 (2020): 71.
25 Chenoweth and Stephan, "Future of nonviolent resistance," 72.
26 Chenoweth and Stephan, "Future of nonviolent resistance," 70.
27 Chenoweth and Stephan, "Future of nonviolent resistance," 72.
28 Martin, "Technology, violence and peace," 14.
29 S. Gallo-Cruz, "Nonviolence beyond the state: International NGOs and local nonviolent mobilization," *International Sociology* 34, no. 6 (2019): 655–674.
30 J. Galtung, "Cultural violence," *Journal of Peace Research* 27, no. 3 (1990): 291–305.
31 P. Uvin, "Global dreams and local anger: From structural to acute violence in a globalizing world," in M. A. Tétreault, R. A. Denemark, K. P. Thomas, and K. Burch (eds.), *Rethinking global political economy: Emerging issues, unfolding odysseys* (New York: Routledge, 2003), 147–162.
32 Galtung, "Cultural violence," 291.
33 Galtung, "Cultural violence," 292.
34 J. Galtung, "An editorial," *Journal of Peace Research* 1, no. 1 (1964): 2.
35 T. M. Turay and L. M. English, "Towards a global culture of peace: A transformative model of peace education," *Journal of Transformative Education* 6, no. 4 (2008): 300.
36 K. Ho, "Structural violence as a human rights violation," *Essex Human Rights Review* 4, no. 2 (2007): 3.
37 J. Galtung, "Violence, peace, and peace research," *Journal of Peace Research* 6, no. 3 (1969): 171.
38 P. Farmer, *Pathologies of power: Health, human rights, and the new war on the poor* (Berkeley: University of California Press, 2005), 40.
39 Galtung, "Cultural violence," 292.
40 J. A. Springs, "The cultural violence of non-violence," *Journal of Mediation and Applied Conflict Analysis* 3, no. 1 (2016): 387.
41 B. Buzan and L. Hansen, *The evolution of international security studies* (Cambridge: Cambridge University Press, 2009); J. A. Vasquez, "Toward a unified strategy for peace education: Resolving the two cultures problem in the classroom," *The Journal of Conflict Resolution* 20, no. 4 (1976), 707–728.
42 Galtung, "Violence, peace, and peace research," 167–191; Galtung, "Cultural violence," 291–305.
43 Galtung, "Violence, peace, and peace research," 167–168.
44 Gene Sharp, "Nonviolent action," in Lester R. Kurtz and Jennifer E. Turpin (eds.), *Encyclopedia of violence, peace, and conflict* 2 (San Diego, CA: Academic Press, 1999), 567.
45 Sharp, *The politics of nonviolent action*.
46 Galtung, "Violence, peace, and peace research," 167–191; Galtung, "Cultural violence," 291–305.
47 J. Galtung, "Peace, war and defense," in *Essays in Peace Research* (Chr. Ejlers Forlag, 1976).
48 B. Charbonneau and G. Parent, "Introduction: Engaging war, creating peace," in B. Charbonneau and G. Parent (eds.), *Peacebuilding, memory and*

reconciliation: Bridging top-down and bottom-up approaches (London and New York: Routledge, 2013), 1–16.
49 R. Mac Ginty, "Hybrid peace: The interaction between top-down and bottom-up peace," *Security Dialogue* 41, no. 4 (2010): 391–412.
50 Chenoweth and Stephan, "Future of nonviolent resistance," 74.
51 J. Pinckney, "Setting the stage for peace processes: The role of nonviolent movements," in C. Buchanan (ed.), *Pioneering peace pathways: Making connections to end violent conflict* (London: Conciliation Resources, 2020), 21–25.

References

Ackerman, P., & DuVall, J. (2000). *A force more powerful: A century of nonviolent conflict*. St. Martin's Press.
Bartkowski, M. (2017, September 27). Do civil resistance movements advance democratization? In *Minds of the movement: An ICNC blog on the people and power of civil resistance*. https://www.nonviolent-conflict.org/blog_post/civil-resistance-movements-advance-democratization/
Bennett, B., & Berenson, T. (2020, November 7). How Donald Trump lost the election. *Time*. https://time.com/5907973/donald-trump-loses-2020-election/
Buzan, B., & Hansen, L. (2009). *The evolution of international security studies*. Cambridge University Press.
Carter, A., Clark, H., & Randle, M. (2006). *People power and protest since 1945: A bibliography of nonviolent action*. Housmans Bookshop.
Carter, A., Clark, H., & Randle, M. (2013). *A guide to civil resistance: A bibliography of people power and nonviolent protest*. Green Print.
Charbonneau, B., & Parent, G. (2012). Introduction: Peacebuilding, healing and reconciliation. In B. Charbonneau & G. Parent (Eds.), *Peacebuilding, memory and reconciliation: Bridging top-down and bottom-up approaches* (pp. 1–16). Routledge.
Chenoweth, E. (2020). Future of nonviolent resistance. *Journal of Democracy*, *31*(3), 69–84.
Chenoweth, E., & Stephan, M. J. (2011). *Why civil resistance works: The strategic logic of nonviolent conflict*. Columbia University Press.
Cobbina, J. (2019). *Hands up, don't shoot: Why the protests in Ferguson and Baltimore matter, and how they changed America*. New York University Press.
Cohen, J. L., & Arato, A. (1994). *Civil society and political theory (Studies in contemporary German social thought)*. MIT Press.
Dudouet, V. (2008). Nonviolent resistance and conflict transformation in power asymmetries. In M. Fischer & B. Schmetzle (Eds.), *Berghof handbook for conflict transformation*. Berghof Research Center for Constructive Conflict Management.
Dudouet, V. (2017). *Powering to peace: Integrated civil resistance and peacebuilding strategies* (ICNC Special Report Series No. 1). International Center on Nonviolent Conflict.
Dukes, E. F. (1999). Structural forces in conflict and conflict resolution in democratic society. In H.-W. Jeong (Ed.), *Conflict resolution: Dynamics, process and structure* (pp. 155–171). Ashgate Publishing.

Farmer, P. (2005). *Pathologies of power: Health, human rights, and the new war on the poor*. University of California Press.

Floresca-Cawagas, V., & Swee-Hin, T. (2008). Institutionalization of nonviolence. In L. Kurtz (Ed.), *Encyclopaedia of violence, peace and conflict* (pp. 1013–1025). Elsevier, Inc.

Gallo-Cruz, S. (2019). Nonviolence beyond the state: International NGOs and local nonviolent mobilization. *International Sociology*, *34*(6), 655–674. https://doi.org/10.1177/0268580919865100

Galtung, J. (1964). An editorial. *Journal of Peace Research*, *1*(1), 1–4.

Galtung, J. (1969). Violence, peace, and peace research. *Journal of Peace Research*, *6*(3), 167–191. https://doi.org/10.1177/002234336900600301

Galtung, J. (1976). *Essays in peace research. Volume 2. Peace, war and defense*. Chr. Ejlers Forlag.

Galtung, J. (1990). Cultural violence. *Journal of Peace Research*, *27*(3), 291–305. https://doi.org/10.1177/0022343390027003005

Hallward, M. J. M., & Mouly, C (2017). Civil resistance in armed conflict: Leveraging nonviolent action to navigate war, oppose violence and confront oppression. *Journal of Peacebuilding & Development*, *12*(3), 1–9. https://doi.org/10.1080/15423166.2017.1376431

Ho, K. (2007). Structural violence as a human rights violation. *Essex Human Rights Review*, *4*(2), 1–17.

Karatnycky, A., & Ackerman, P. (2005). *How freedom is won: From civic resistance to durable democracy*. Freedom House.

King, M. E. (2008). Nonviolent struggle in Africa: Essentials of knowledge and teaching. *Africa Peace and Conflict Journal*, *1*(1), 19–44.

Lederach, J. P. (1995). *Preparing for peace: Conflict transformation across cultures*. Syracuse University Press.

López Martínez, M. (2012). *Ni paz, ni guerra, sino todo lo contrario: Ensayos sobre defensa y resistencia civil*. Granada: Educatori.

Mac Ginty, R. (2010). Hybrid peace: The interaction between top-down and bottom-up peace. *Security Dialogue*, *41*(4), 391–412. https://doi.org/10.1177/0967010610374312

Martin, B. (2008). Technology, violence and peace. In L. Kurtz (Editor-in-chief), *Encyclopedia of violence, peace, & conflict* (2nd ed., pp. 2045–2055). Elsevier, Inc.

Martinez, M. L. (2012). *Ni paz, ni guerra, sino todo lo contrario. Ensayos sobre defensa y resistencia civil*. Granada Educatori.

McCarthy, R. M., & Sharp, G. (1997). *Nonviolent action: A research guide*. Garland Press.

Pinckney, J. (2020). Setting the stage for peace processes: The role of nonviolent movements. In C. Buchanan (Ed.), *Pioneering peace pathways: Making connections to end violent conflict* (pp. 21–25). Accord 29.

Randle, M. (1994). *Civil resistance*. Fontana Press.

Roberts, A. (2009). Introduction. In A. Roberts & T. G. Ash (Eds.), *Civil resistance and power politics: The experience of non-violent action from Gandhi to the present* (pp. 1–24). Oxford University Press.

Roberts, A., & Ash, T. G. (2009). *Civil resistance & power politics: The experience of non-violent action from Gandhi to the present*. Oxford University Press.

Schock, K. (2005). *Unarmed insurrections: People power movements in nondemocracies*. University of Minnesota Press.

Serhan, Y. (2020, August 26). What Belarus learned from the rest of the world. *The Atlantic*. https://www.theatlantic.com/international/archive/2020/08/belaurus-protest-tactics-hong-kong/615454/

Sharp, G. (1973). *The politics of nonviolent action. Part two: The methods of nonviolent action*. Porter Sargent Publishers.

Sharp, G. (1999). Nonviolent action. In L. R. Kurtz & J. E. Turpin (Eds.), *Encyclopedia of violence, peace, and conflict* (Vol. 2, pp. 567–74). Academic Press.

Springs, J. A. (2015). Structural and cultural violence in religion and peacebuilding. In A. Omer, R. S. Appleby, & D. Little (Eds.), *The Oxford handbook of religion, conflict, and peacebuilding* (pp. 146–179). Oxford University Press.

Springs, J. A. (2016). The cultural violence of non-violence. *Journal of Mediation and Applied Conflict Analysis*, *3*(1), 382–396.

Swee-Hin, T., & Floresca-Cawagas, V. (2008). Institutionalization of non-violence. In L. Kurtz (Editor-in-chief), *Encyclopedia of violence, peace, & conflict* (pp. 1013–1025). Elsevier, Inc.

Turay, T. M., & English, L. M. (2008). Towards a global culture of peace: A transformative model of peace education. *Journal of Transformative Education*, *6*(4), 286–301. https://doi.org/10.1177/1541344608330602

Uvin, P. (2003). Global dreams and local anger: From structural to acute violence in a globalizing world. In M. A. Tétreault, R. A. Denemark, K. P. Thomas, & K. Burch (Eds.), *Rethinking global political economy: Emerging issues, unfolding odysseys* (pp. 147–162). Routledge.

Vasquez, J. A. (1976). Toward a unified strategy for peace education: Resolving the two cultures problem in the classroom. *The Journal of Conflict Resolution*, *20*(4), 707–728. https://doi.org/10.1177/002200277602000407

3 Polish nonviolent resistance against foreign occupation 1795–1918

A post-revisionist perspective

Jacek Lubecki

3.1 Introduction

In the wake of the "color revolutions" of the 2000s and the Arab Spring revolutions of the early 2010s, there has been an understandable explosion of scholarship on nonviolent resistance, including its history. A paradigmatic volume in this wave of historical writing was a 2013 work titled *Recovering Nonviolent History: Civil Resistance in Liberation Struggles*, edited by Professor Maciej Bartkowski, which presented a series of 15 case studies of nonviolent struggles for national liberation varying from Sub-Saharan Africa (Ghana, Zambia, and Mozambique) to the Middle East (Algeria, Egypt, Iran, and Palestine), Europe (Hungary, Kosovo, and Poland), Asia and Oceania (Burma, Bangladesh, and West Papua), and the Americas (the United States and Cuba) and covering history all the way from the 18th century (the American revolution) to today (Palestine, West Papua).[1] The volume was explicitly revisionist and came with two key claims: first, nonviolent struggles for independence have been deliberately and unfairly marginalized in national memorializations and official histories of all the examined nations, and in all cases, nonviolent elements of struggles for independence have been crucial for the eventual success of the efforts, especially for national identity formation and the institutional success of the newly emerging states.

This chapter in the current volume is indented to be a post-revisionist response to *Recovering Nonviolent History*, specifically to the book's chapter on Poland,[2] authored by Bartkowski himself. Using the Polish chapter as an example of the type of scholarship presented in the book, I will claim that:

1 Regardless of its introductory claims, *Recovering Nonviolent History* presents decontextualized and selective reading of the national histories, often distorting and obscuring the roles that violent resistance,

nonviolent resistance, and collaboration with occupying powers played in the struggles for independence.
2 The key concept of the accounts—namely, what counts as "nonviolent resistance"—is not defined and used consistently in Bartkowski's own chapter.
3 Based on the Polish example, it is also not true that memories and history of nonviolent resistance are routinely suppressed and marginalized by later national politics. Instead, like all history, memories of nonviolent resistance are subject to instrumentalization in function of subsequent political developments, which sometimes celebrate and sometimes marginalize particular historical memories in function of current politics. In other words, there is no deterministic logic that suppresses memories of any particular type of resistance in later national memorializations.

The chapter is organized in the following way. First, the chapter will present a broad panorama of the Polish case in its full historical context and situate Bartkowski's account of Polish nonviolent resistance in this context. Second, the chapter will critically reexamine Bartkowski's specific claims about Polish nonviolent resistance and its consequences. Finally, the chapter will draw broader conclusions from the post-revisionist claims.

3.2 Poland under partitions (1795–1918) and Polish nonviolent resistance

An early modern Polish state called the Commonwealth of Two Nations (Polish and Lithuanian) existed roughly between the 15th and 18th centuries and featured proto-liberal institutions that extended substantial political rights and civil liberties to the dominant gentry (*szlachta*, also translated as nobility) status group. The state also featured a brutal subjugation of serfs and exclusion of non-noble strata from power. The commonwealth was violently destroyed in the course of the second half of the 18th century by its imperial absolutist and militaristic neighbors: Russia, Prussia, and Austria, a process finally accomplished by 1795. The final moments of the commonwealth were marked with dramatic acts of Polish resistance: violent and nonviolent. In 1791, the commonwealth's parliament (its lower chamber called *Sejm* and the upper chamber, the Senate) created Europe's first modern written constitution and advanced a series of reforms intended to democratize and strengthen the state; this led to a joint Russian and Prussian military intervention, partition, and the reduction of Poland to a status of a small Russian-dominated puppet state in 1792.

In response, between 1793 and 1794, Tadeusz Kościuszko, a hero of the American Revolution known for his radical egalitarian and republican ideals, led a violent Polish insurrection intended to be a revolutionary "people's war" against all three partitioning powers. After its defeat, the period between 1795 and 1918 was punctuated by Polish armed attempts to win total independence, often coupled to social radicalism. This was done in alliance with Napoleon (1796–1814), in a war/insurgency against Russia (1830–1831), against all three empires (1846), against Prussia and Austria (1848), against Russia in the January 1863 uprising (1863–1864), and against Russia, again, in the revolution of 1905–1907. In-between these violent uprisings, the period of partitions featured unarmed attempts to cultivate the national life in all three partition areas. Finally, the geopolitical outcomes of World War I, which featured the collapse of all three partitioning empires, coupled with nonviolent political, civilian, and military activities by various Polish factions delivered Poland's full independence by the end of 1918.

Like all such struggles, the Polish one created its critical dilemmas and endless debates and clashes regarding the respective virtues of different forms of armed resistance vs. nonviolent resistance, and resistance vs. collaboration with the occupying powers. These debates and dilemmas have been faithfully reproduced in discourses, dilemmas, and debates of other nations in similar circumstances. Indeed, it is stunning how all national movements faced with similar circumstances of foreign occupation often go through the same phases of struggles, ask the same questions, and engage in the same strategic debates while often being seemingly and blissfully unaware that all of it happened before to other nations.

In a stylized form, the debates pitted, on the one hand, violent romantics who celebrated violent resistance as preserving and advancing the national spirit regardless of the typically catastrophic effects that actual failed violent resistance has on the substance of national life. On the other side, we find nonviolent pragmatists, who saw most romantic actions as unrelieved foolishness. The pragmatist faction, in turn, can be divided between pragmatic collaborationists and nonviolent resisters, just like the "violent" strategists have their factions: insurrectionists, partisans of protracted popular war, pragmatic manipulators of geostrategy, and so on. The divisions on tactics and strategy were often along factional and partisan lines, resulting in bitter and sometimes violently negotiated clashes within nationalist movements: Fatah vs. Hamas in Palestine, Józef Piłsudski vs. Roman Dmowski in Poland, and so on. Bitter divisions, and not unity, indeed, were the hallmark of the entire Polish nationalist movement during the partitions period, as similar divisions had been very much in evidence in the Zionist, Indian independence, Palestinian, and other similar movements.

In a 2013 pioneering chapter, "Forging the Polish Nation Nonviolently, 1860–1900s," Professor Bartkowski described Polish nonviolent resistance against foreign occupation following the failure of 1863–1864 uprising. He focused on particular episodes of what he classified as "Polish nonviolent resistance" in all three partitioning powers (Austria-Hungary, Germany, and Russia) and linked his account of the Polish history to revisionist claims to the entire book—namely, that in institutionalized national memories of countries liberated by struggles for independence in modern times, ranging from the United States in the 18th century to Palestine today, violent resistance is privileged at the expense of nonviolent resistance, the memory and practice of which need to be recovered in academic scholarship and national consciousness.

In the context of the flourishing 2010s scholarship and literature on nonviolent resistance, which indeed can no longer claim to be marginalized in academic discourse (see Appendix A), why do we need another chapter on Polish nonviolent resistance against foreign occupation tackling roughly the same theme as Bartkowski's work? I claim in my chapter that Bartkowski's chapter and perhaps the broader scholarship on "nonviolent resistance" is in need of corrections and revision, if the scholarship wants to overcome its activist roots and present the truly nuanced and fully contextualized account of nonviolent resistance in cases like the Polish one. As I will show later, Bartkowski's chapter includes a fair amount of conceptual confusion and factual inaccuracies, which end up presenting a partially flawed account of the Polish struggle for independence and the role of nonviolent resistance in that struggle. Specifically, the chapter fails to define what is "nonviolent resistance"; instead, it focuses selectively and unsystematically on a number of nonviolent Polish societal activities that only in retrospect and with the benefit of hindsight strengthened Polish national consciousness in the face of foreign oppression. Besides, the chapter presents a decontextualized account of selected episodes of "nonviolent resistance" and does not really get an answer to the question of how Poland gained independence and the role that nonviolent resistance played in that struggle.

There is no doubt that Bartkowski's work and the other chapters presented in the volume that he edited have served a useful and important role of revisionist scholarship by presenting an alternative and true narratives of nonviolent struggles for the independence of the respective nations. The flaws of the accounts, as illustrated by Bartkowski's chapter, are typical of revisionism—with a focus on debunking previously dominant narratives and animated by a desire, rooted in activism, to present nonviolent resistance as important, the scholarship takes conceptual and factual shortcuts that end up presenting a distorted and simplified vision of complex historical realities. As always in historical and social science scholarship, revisionism is in need of post-revisionism. Accordingly, my chapter is not just about the Polish case, but uses the case to create broader conclusions about the scholarship, theories, and accounts of nonviolent resistance across the world. Specifically, I claim that the scholarship is in need of more rigorous conceptualization, richer contextualization, and more careful attention to historical detail to create more richly textured and nuanced—and therefore, more accurate—accounts of cases like Poland. Most importantly, the role of historical contingency and collaboration with occupying or established powers need to be given their due, alongside accounts of nonviolent resistance, to explain how real struggles for national liberation actually happen. Otherwise, for instance, current struggles for national liberation, such as the Kurdish or Palestinian ones, are seen against the background of idealized and distorted history of previous cases, which appear to be "morally pure" instead of their real and complex messiness.

3.3 Context, collaboration, violence, and nonviolence. Examining the specific episodes

Bartkowski begins his narrative of the Polish case with the failure of the national uprising of January 1863 (lasted from January 1863 to spring 1864 and was aimed against Russia), which according to him was the last great national attempt to gain independence through violence between 1864 and 1914. This notion itself is a bit of a distortion—the uprising did not end military attempts to gain independence as amply documented in Janusz Wojtasik 1987 (revisionist) monograph *Idea walki zbrojnej o niepodległość Polski, 1864–1907* ("Ideas on armed struggles for Poland's independence 1864–1907").[3] In turn, the 1905–1907 period featured a violent nationalist and social revolution in the Russian partition of Poland as part of the Russian revolution,[4] while the period between 1907 and 1914 was rife with insurrectionary military planning (see Appendix B).[5] Especially Józef Piłsudski, a leader of a faction of the Polish Socialist Party, which violently participated in the revolution of 1905–1907, continued his anti-Russian activity from the Austrian partition of Poland, supported in this endeavor by Austrian and German intelligence services.[6] The period of World War I, finally, featured strong militarized efforts to gain independence, mostly in collaboration with partitioning powers, the most famous of which are Piłsudski's legions, which emerged after the failure of his original idea of a mass nationalist uprising against Russia in advance of Austro-Hungarian and German armies invading Russian territories of Poland in 1914.[7] It is true though that between 1864 and 1905, ideas of violent resistance were not hegemonic in Polish nationalist thought, and Bartkowski's focus on this period and actions undertaken is warranted.

However, the partially arbitrary periodization presented by Bartkowski presents another problem by decontextualizing the story of the 1864–1905 period from its broader geopolitical and historical frame. Bartkowski seems to be operating with a simplified image of Polish history based on a notion that in 1795 Poland lost independence; in 1918 the country regained it; and between 1795 and 1864 ideas and practices of violent resistance were hegemonic, to be replaced between 1864 and 1914 by more constructive nonviolent resistance, leading to Polish independence in 1918. This narrative's frame is too distorted and simplified to be given justice to complexities of the struggle and the role that collaboration and historical contingency played in the process. Interestingly enough, in the preface to the entire volume (see Appendix C), Bartkowski claims that nuanced and fully contextualized accounts of the role of nonviolence in the respective national cases will be given, a dictum that he does not follow in his own chapter. So the question remains: How do we properly contextualize Bartkowski's narrative and the whole question of "Polish nonviolent resistance"?

In 1795, upon the failure of Kościuszko's uprising, the partitioning powers signed the St. Petersburg Convention of 1797, which besides erasing Poland as a territorial state, also committed them to erase the very name of "Poland" or "Polish Kingdom" and any traces of Polish nationalism. This project was a failure from the very beginning and decisively crumbled within a decade when, between 1805 and 1807, Napoleon defeated all three partitioning powers and created a semi-sovereign Polish state called "the Duchy of Warsaw" (*Księstwo Warszawskie*) endowed with fully national armed forces and state administration and committed to the flourishing of Polish national culture and society. The duchy was enlarged in 1809, when it defeated an invading Austrian army and took over Polish territories occupied by Austria. In 1812 Polish armed forces represented the second largest contingent after the French in Napoleon's *Grande Armée*. Significantly, Napoleon called his war against Russia "the Second Polish War," with the goal of recreating the pre-partition Polish Kingdom, which was indeed formally proclaimed in June 1812 in Warsaw. In a twist of historical fate, Napoleon's defeat between 1812 and 1815 did not lead to return to the 1797 *status quo* of the complete suppression of Poland. To the contrary, the liberal Tzar Alexander I of Russia, impressed by Polish national efforts under Napoleon, decided to continue a form of Polish statehood based on the (diminished) boundaries of the Duchy of Warsaw. It was renamed the Kingdom of Poland and linked to Russia in a dynastic union whereby the tzar of Russia was also crowned (separately, in Warsaw) as king of Poland. The kingdom had a separate constitution, a fully Polish administration, army, cultural institutions, and boundaries separate from Russia proper. In the meantime, Polish areas of the Prussian partition were given autonomy in the form of a Grand Duchy of Poznań, while the most important Polish city in the former Austrian areas, Kraków, was given autonomy as a "free city" under the supervision of all three partitioning powers. Polish cultural, social, and economic life were permitted to flourish in all three areas, but especially in the Kingdom of Poland, which was given everything short of full sovereignty in terms of Polish national existence, which was under no threat of disappearing.

The above detail is important, because it fills up the "black hole" left behind by Bartkowski's truncated narrative that gives the impression that the Polish national life prior to 1864 was somehow fully suppressed and dominated by violent attempts at independence. In fact, violence was interspersed with periods of peaceful Polish national institution-building often undertaken, not in resistance against, but actually in collaboration with partitioning powers, especially Russia, between 1815 and 1830. Moreover, what was "collaboration" and what is "resistance" becomes hopelessly blurred in the context of the reality, like the Polish Kingdom from 1815 to 1830. For instance, when Prince Ksawery Drucki-Lubecki, the kingdom's minister of the treasury, and an economic administrator who was clearly dedicated to Polish national development in faithful alliance with Russia, dramatically reversed the catastrophic fiscal shape of the kingdom launched it on the path of industrial and agricultural development and fought a successful trade war against Prussia, was it resistance or collaboration? In retrospect, the internal and autonomous development of the Polish economy led by him was clearly a coup for the eventual emergence of a modern Polish state and nation, and today, the prince is celebrated in Polish patriotic national memory.[8] It is much less discussed that when the uprising of 1830 broke out, Drucki-Lubecki went to St. Petersburg and bitterly opposed the insurrection, which ended the semi-sovereignty of the Polish Kingdom. Examples like this expose a conceptual problem within the "civil" or "nonviolent" resistance literature—namely, a lack of precision in defining what counts as nonviolent resistance. In abstract, Bartkowski defines "nonviolence" resistance in the following way:

> A form of political conflict in which ordinary people choose to stand up to oppressive structures—be it occupation, colonialism, or unjust practices of government—with the use of various tactics of nonviolent action such as strikes, boycotts, protests, and civil disobedience. Such methods include not only overt confrontational actions, but also subtler forms of cultural resistance or seemingly apolitical work of autonomous associations and parallel institution building. Whether overt or tacit, nonviolent forms of resistance are a popular expression of

people's collective determination to withdraw their cooperation from the powers that be.[9]

In her seminal introduction to the special issue of *Journal of Peace Studies* dedicated to nonviolent resistance, Erica Chenoweth, in turn, defines "nonviolent resistance" in the following way:

> We define nonviolent resistance as the application of unarmed civilian power using nonviolent methods such as protests, strikes, boycotts, and demonstrations, without using or threatening physical harm against the opponents. Civilians challenging the state through nonviolent struggle employ irregular political tactics, working outside the defined and accepted channels for political participation defined by the state. As will become clear from the contributions of this special issue, ordinary people use nonviolent resistance to pursue a wide variety of goals, from challenging entrenched autocrats to seeking territorial self-determination to contesting widespread discriminatory practices.[10]

Let us notice that, while similar, these two definitions are not identical. The "irregular political tactics, working outside the defined and accepted channels for political participation defined by the state" restriction is not present in Bartkowski's definition, but both definitions include references to "ordinary people," which seems to exclude political elites. Chenoweth refers to "irregular political tactics" while Bartkowski refers to "seemingly apolitical work of autonomous associations and parallel institution building." Both definitions exclude physical violence against "opponents," but in a footnoted reference, Bartkowski counts destruction of property as a form of nonviolent resistance. It is pretty clear that in the light of these fairly narrow definitions, no Polish activities that I describe above, no matter how much they contributed to the Polish national cause, should count as "nonviolent resistance" because they were either violent or pursued by the elite through "normal political channels."

However, let us see how, in practice, the civil resistance literature operationalized the definitions of nonviolent resistance. Referring to post-1864 Polish realities, Bartkowski himself counts the following three Polish groups activities as "nonviolent resistance":

1 Educational, organizational, and cultural (legal) efforts to endow Polish peasantry/rural lower classes of the Austro-Hungarian (since 1866) partition of Poland (Galicia) with Polish national consciousness.
2 Polish efforts to resisting Germanization in the German partition of Poland after 1871. This included boycotts and school strikes (illegal)

against Germanized, anti-Catholic schools, a creation of Polish agrarian and financial (legal) institutions to resist German efforts to buy Polish land, and educational (legal) efforts to advance Polish-language literacy and education.

3   Illegal efforts from 1880s to 1905 to create a parallel Polish educational system in the Russian partition of Poland, subject to Russification since the 1870s.

How do these particular examples fit within the framework of Polish political history and definitional issues just raised? Let us reprise our narrative of Polish national history under the partitions and see the problems with Bartkowski's definition, narrative, and examples are illustrative of general issues with civil resistance literature.

After 1831 the Kingdom of Poland, the key part of the Russian partition, was deprived of many of its autonomous institutions (the military, universities, its parliament) and subjected to harsh Russian military rule but still maintained its Polish lower-level administration and institutional, economic, and political existence separate from the Russian Empire. The Russian occupation was very harsh, and when in 1846, a Polish network of revolutionary exiles led by Ludwik Mierosławski planned a general national uprising (which was to be accompanied by the abolition of serfdom and a people's war in Poland), the plan completely failed in Russia. Simultaneously, this incompetent plot ended up with a wave of arrests in the Prussian partition and in a tragedy in the Austrian partition, where Polish-speaking peasants, in an act of class retribution, actually massacred the Polish nobility planning the uprising. Two years later, in 1848, similar efforts ended up with military defeats and an end to all autonomous Polish institutions in the Prussian and Austrian parts of Poland. In the meantime, the harsh military rule in the Polish Kingdom relaxed a bit, and by 1857, there were attempts by Russia to liberalize its reign over the Polish subjects. By 1860, this led to a full-blown effort to resurrect the pre-1830 Polish autonomy (minus an army) in the Polish Kingdom, led on the Polish side by a faction of conservative but patriotic landed aristocracy under the leadership of Margrave Aleksander Wielopolski. His efforts were successful, as a far-reaching autonomy was granted again to the kingdom in 1860, while Wielopolski himself, in 1862, was nominated by the tzar to be the head of the civilian administration of the kingdom.[11]

It was precisely in reaction to Wielopolski's efforts that radical Polish underground was born and plotted and executed a massive violent uprising against the Russian rule starting in January 1863. Explicitly knowing the gap in the military forces involved, what was sought by the insurgents was "rivers of blood" that would prevent Wielopolski's effort at a national compromise and existence of autonomous Poland as a part of Russia (see Appendix D). Then, in the midst of the uprising, England, France, and Austria intervened on behalf of Polish independence, to be rebuked by Russia. Unwilling to go to war against Russia on behalf of Poland, the intervening powers stood down, and the uprising was drowned, as intended, in "a sea of blood," while the Polish Kingdom was abolished by 1872. Partially as a result of uprising, though, the Russians terminated serfdom in Poland at conditions advantageous to the Polish peasantry and endowed Polish village communities with substantial powers of self-government, seeing in Polish peasants the social basis of Russian rule in Poland, as contrary to the Polish gentry and urban classes. Almost simultaneously, the 1871 German unification resulted in harsh anti-Polish denationalizing measures in the Prussian partition of Poland. Across the board, by 1872, the Polish national cause seemed to have reached its nadir, and this is roughly the point when Bartkowski starts his narrative.

However, in an act of historical irony and perhaps justice, while national oppression and repression of Polishness was dramatically intensified in the German (Prussian) and Russian partitions of Poland, deprived of all autonomy and subjected to denationalizing policies, a reverse process happened in the Austrian partition of Poland. After defeats in Italy (1859) and in a war against Prussia (1866), the tottering Austrian Empire decided to embark on a dramatic course of conservative liberalization. Between 1860 and 1867, the state was transformed into a loose confederacy of Austria and Hungary, while within the Austrian part, a fairly liberal constitutional order was created that, among others, conceded a far-reaching autonomy and self-rule to the Polish partition formally known as the Kingdom of Galicia and Lodomeria, or Galicia for short. This meant, in practice, that Polish landed aristocracy, backed by conservative intelligentsia, received almost total local political power in the province, which was met with their enthusiastic loyalism.

Soon, with Poles being seen as the most loyal element of the Austrian monarchy, Polish aristocrats, like Alfred Józef Potocki (1870–1871) and Kazimierz Badeni (1895–1897) became prime ministers of the entire Austrian part of the empire. Polish culture, language, autonomous institutions, education and religion, and transnational efforts at resistance and independence aimed against Russia (primarily, these were supported by Austria) and Germany (tolerated by Austria) flourished. In the meantime, any Polish nationalist resistance against Austria disappeared, to be replaced by gratitude and loyalty even among radical left-wing movements. Galicia was seen as a potential "Polish Piedmont," a semi-autonomous springboard for full independence, to be achieved through and in alliance with Austro-Hungary.

In the words of one Polish historian, Poles in Galicia missed only one thing: full sovereignty.[12]

It is in the context of Galician autonomy, Austrian liberal institutions, and a complete absence of any threat of denationalization of the Polish population that emerged a Galician democratic political culture visible to this day in Polish politics.[13] This was a result of a complex set of circumstances, which, besides the already described institutional factors, featured a specific, mostly rural and agricultural and poor, but modernizing political economy as well as Galicia's complex national politics. Precisely because of the absence of national oppression, class factors took prominence in Polish-on-Polish political struggles in the region, as long disenfranchised and oppressed, poor, and land-hungry Polish peasants, and then, an emerging working class took on the Polish landed aristocracy and urban bourgeoisie.[14] In complex ways this conflict superimposed itself on a national conflict, this time also featuring Polish landed aristocracy as oppressors of mostly Ukrainian/Rusyn peasants who demographically dominated the Eastern part of Galicia. Given that the Polish autonomous Galicia gave the control of local institutions to Polish upper classes, in the conflict of Polish lower classes against Polish upper classes, the former took advantage of the fact that Austrian national institutions—elections, civil rights, and liberties—were more liberal, democratic, and open than local institutions dominated by the Polish aristocracy. Besides stimulating enfranchisement of Polish lower classes, perhaps unintentionally, the Austrian polity was also sympathetic to the Ukrainian national cause, partially in function of geopolitics—intending to use both Polish and Ukrainian nationalisms against Russia.

In this context, Polish left-wing, peasant and workers' parties and movements, which deemphasized nationalism and emphasized a common cause of fighting Polish aristocracy with Ukrainian peasants, actually served the broader Austrian national interest by creating a cross-national Polish-Ukrainian lower-class alliance aimed against Polish upper classes. As a result, tolerated or even encouraged by Austrian state, class-based peasant and worker Polish parties flourished in increasingly liberalized political life in Galicia. Still, this was not accomplished easily or peacefully: local Polish upper class, which dominated oligarchical Galician institutions, fought tooth and nail against class-based movements or Polish or Ukrainian working classes and peasantry, which fought back with strikes, demonstrations, protests, pickets, and marches—tools of civil resistance certainly, but in the Galician case, aimed at class rather than national liberation.[15]

Bartkowski, in his chapter, presents educational, cultural, and political enfranchisement of Polish peasantry of Galicia at the end of 19th century as a part of Polish "nonviolent resistance" against "foreign occupation" that somehow prevented looming "de-nationalisation" of the Polish population of the province. A part of these Polish-speaking and Catholic peasants' process of class liberation was indeed an acquisition of their own subjective understanding of their Polishness in the sense of gaining a sense of their own worth as self-aware Polish peasants fighting for their rights and interests against oppressive Polish upper classes, which often blocked lower-class efforts at self-education.[16] This, however, had nothing to do with any "nonviolent resistance against foreign occupation" in the context of "a threat of de-nationalization" of which there was none. Moreover, in the context of the class struggles, Polish upper classes often started using Polish nationalism as a tool of pacifying Polish lower classes a tool of national cross-class solidarity.

Two events fit into that strategy, and they were both described by Bartkowski as episodes of "nonviolent resistance": one was a mass and lavish celebration of the anniversaries of Kościuszko's uprising of 1793, specifically of the 1794 Battle of Racławice, which featured Polish serf, scythe-armed peasant-soldiers, defeating Russian soldiers, while the second was a similar celebration of Polish king Jan Sobieski's victory over the Ottomans at Vienna in 1683. No doubt, the presence of Polish patriotic peasant-soldiers at Racławice, fighting for Polish independence, could be thus used to bind Polish peasantry to the Polish national cause, whereas for the Catholic peasants, the victory of Christendom over Muslims in 1683 in the context of the last great Polish military victory in history could serve the cause of national pride and self-identification as Polish. However, these events, sponsored by the regional Polish state and its political establishment fit no definition of "nonviolent resistance" as established by Bartkowski or Chenoweth: these were official state-sponsored events that celebrated violent nationalistic episodes and served primarily the function of upper class hegemony, as an actual struggle for independence against Austria was on nobody's mind. Moreover, for Bartkowski, who spends a good part of his book and chapter decrying the hegemony of nationalistic violence in Polish historical memory, to evoke two events that celebrated precisely nationalistic violence is ironic, to say the least. In the meantime, he completely overlooks rampant mass nonviolent resistance between 1880 and 1914 in Galicia, which was mostly aimed against Polish upper classes and their political hegemony. Thus, the context and essence of what was going on in Galicia in his description of the rise of national Polish peasantry of Galicia as "nonviolent resistance against foreign occupation" is absent. As it is, the Galician case simply does not fit his narrative or definition of "nonviolent resistance."

In contrast to the Galician case, Bartkowski's characterization of Polish nonviolent resistance against German (Prussian) and Russian denationalization efforts does not pose the fundamental conceptual and factual historical problems so obvious in his description of the Galician case. In the German case, indeed, after 1871 the German state launched a campaign aimed to eradicate Polish ownership of land, national consciousness, and even language and religion from the Polish regions of Germany, and this effort was nonviolently resisted by the Polish population in forms that fit the standard definition of civil resistance. However, and this is where Bartkowski misses the broader context of the struggle, this German state-led effort was a part of a generalized campaign to subdue all potentially "disloyal" elements of the newly unified German state, which, for Protestant and hegemonic Prussian elite, included not just Poles, but more importantly, all Catholics. The term *Kulturkampf* ("war over culture")[17] as an episode in German political history actually means struggle against the influence of the Catholic Church in German political and cultural life—and, since Poles were mostly Catholic, and had the extra "sin" of being Polish, this broader struggle was waged especially viciously and coupled to denationalization in the Polish provinces.[18] However, this also meant that the Poles had the sympathy of German Catholics and the entire world's Catholic public opinion. In fact, this whole context is missing from Bartkowski's account, and one does not quite know why, as it could enrich his case, which is fundamentally sound.

Bartkowski's description of Polish resistance against Germanization as coupled to the general thrust of his claim that memory of nonviolent resistance is everywhere marginalized in favor of violent resistance is problematic for another reason—namely, it is simply not true that Polish nonviolent resistance against German encroachment between 1871 and 1918 was later marginalized in Polish national memory. As it is, institutionalized Polish memory has always celebrated all resistance, violent and nonviolent, against foreign occupations, but the particular pride of place has belonged to nonviolent resistance against the Germans, celebrated in novels (Bolesław Prus's famous novel *The Outpost*[19]) the symbolism of Drzymała's wagon,[20] poetry (Maria Konopnicka's poem "Rota" or "The Oath," later turned into the second most popular Polish patriotic song (see Appendix F)), film (a lavishly funded all-star TV series of 13 parts titled *Najdłusza wojna nowoczesnej Europy—The Longest War of Modern Europe* [see Appendix G]), monuments (a monument to striking children of Września, who refused to take their religious education in German, erected in 1975 [see Appendix H]), and so on. Especially during the communist period of Polish history, when full-on anti-German Polish nationalism was a very important element of communist claim to Polish patriotism (see Appendix I) and ideological hegemony, lavish resources, countless memorializations, and entire institutions[21] were dedicated to the celebration of Polish nonviolent resistance against the Germans. This is simply a fact of history, which, again, does not fit into Bartkowski's preconceived notions, and is therefore simply skipped in his chapter.

In the Russian partition case, Bartkowski's claim that Polish efforts to create a parallel illegal educational system between the 1870s and 1905 to counter the official Russifying schools represented an important act of Polish nonviolent resistance is sound. Indeed, the Tzarist government launched, after the 1863 uprising, a full-blown effort to denationalize the Polish nation through fully Russified institutions, which included Russian-language-only compulsory education, aimed at depriving Polish children of their language and culture. This was countered by the Polish civil society by efforts to create a private and parallel educational system, which was widespread and defeated the Russian efforts.

What is missing from Bartkowski's otherwise accurate account is the full historical story of the Polish struggle to counter Russification, especially as the Russian Empire started liberalizing after 1905. In the context of the Russian revolution of 1905–1907, which featured a panoply of violent and nonviolent forms of anti-Tzarist resistance, the Poles of the Russian partition launched a boycott of Russian educational institutions, which paralyzed them between 1905 and 1907.[22] To replace the Russian state schools, taking advantage of the liberalization of the period, Poles created their own—this time, legal—educational institutions. These, in turn, were mostly banned, as the reaction and repression rose again with the failure of the revolution in 1907. However, the Russian repression of Polishness never returned to the pre-1905 status quo: private and vocational Polish-language educational institutions remained legal, and some Polish-language education was allowed in state schools. This was in the context of the looming conflict with Germany and Austria, in which Russia wanted to use the tool of Polish nationalism (anti-German, especially) just as much as its Germanic enemies wanted to use Polish anti-Russian nationalism. A pro-Polish faction emerged in this context within the Tzarist bureaucracy, pushing for further concession to Polish nationalism. Poles reciprocated with the emergence of a powerful national movement and party, known as National Democracy (*endecja*), which sought a path for the national liberation of Poland in alliance with Russia against Germany, considered the worst existential enemy of Polishness. Therefore, by 1914, collaboration, not resistance, again became a chief means of the Polish fight for independence in the Russian partition of Poland.

So how did Poland actually regain independence, and what role did nonviolent resistance play in that process? This story is completely missing from Bartkowski's chapter, and for a good reason: while what he describes and defines as nonviolent resistance in the German and Russian partitions in Poland definitely played a dramatic role in preserving Polishness in the face of German and Russian (but not Austrian, as there were none) denationalization efforts after the 1870s to approximately 1905–1914, these events played only a tangential role in the complex politics of the Polish cause in the 1914–1918 period. One facet of that period that completely does not fit into Bartkowski's narrative is a fact that pretty much all Polish serious political forces aligned (or oriented themselves) with one or the other side in the war (so, Austria-Hungary and Germany or Russia and its Western allies) to regain independence: that is, Polish independence was to be gained in collaboration with, not in resistance against one or more of the partitioning powers. Second, the contingencies of the war led to the situation in which both sides of the war themselves started promoting Polish nationalism and the cause of Polish freedom (manipulatively defined, of course) as their war goals, thus finally nullifying the enslaving tripartite consensus of the partition period.

Paradoxically enough, it was Germany—the great enemy of Polishness in its own areas of Poland—that became the first champion of Polish sovereignty and statehood in the areas of the former Russian partition that Germany (and Austria-Hungary, the quickly fading and weak German ally) conquered in 1915. As a result, on November 5, 1916, the German and Austro-Hungarian authorities proclaimed the creation of an autonomous (the term used was "self-governing") Polish Kingdom united into an alliance with the Central Powers and endowed with all the trappings of sovereignty including a military force. This was followed and preceded with a slew of measures that amounted to Polish nation-building in the territories of the former (Russian-dominated) Polish Kingdom: a Polish central government and institutions of local self-government were created, Polish schools (including a University in Warsaw) were reopened, Polish national symbolism (the red and white flag, for instance) took over the Polish street, and Germans presented themselves as champions of Polish independence.[23] Not to be outdone, the Russians, still under the tzar, proclaimed "free Poland" to be their war goal, while in 1917 both the liberal Provisional government and the Bolshevik government of Russia renounced Russian territories of Poland and proclaimed Polish independence as recognized by Russia.[24] Thus, when President Wilson also proclaimed independent Poland to be one of the Western allies' war goals, he was simply confirming the existing consensus of both sides of the war: all were for Polish independence; the question was only when, how, and what shape it will take.

In the context of these monumental historical contingencies, Polish nationalist forces aligned themselves, as I already mentioned, with one or the other side of the war, but for most of them, these alliances were contingent and breakable depending on what and how much each side of the war was willing to do for the Polish cause—in other words, this was the historical moment when the price of Polish political support was to be bought, in a bidding war, with greater and greater concessions to the Polish national cause. Still, it did not prevent bitter divisions within the Polish national camp, symbolized by the respective figures of Józef Piłsudski, who initially wanted to gain Polish independence in alliance with Central Powers and against Russia, and Roman Dmowski, who wanted to achieve the same goal in alliance with Russia and the Western Powers. As it is, both orientations' original plans crumbled: the German concessions proved to be insincere and insufficient (especially as exemplified in the March 1918 Brest-Litowsk peace treaty with Russia and its aftermath), while Russia simply crumbled in 1917 and was of no consequence for the final settlement of the Polish issue. Thus, in 1918, all Polish nationalist forces converged on the option of gaining independence in alliance with Western Powers and against Central Powers, which occupied, at the time, all Polish territories. A mass Polish, mostly nonviolent, movement accomplished that goal during the months of October and November in 1918 as the occupying forces of Germany and Austria-Hungary simply melted away.[25] This story is completely missing from Bartkowski's narrative.

Bartkowski makes a big deal out of supposed institutional and cultural legacies of Polish nonviolent resistance in terms of later patterns of existence of the newly independent Polish state. Specifically, he stated that:

> Without nonviolent resistance, Poles could not have taken charge of their national destiny after World War I or changed the geopolitical situation in their favor during the 1980s. It would have been equally implausible to integrate partitioned lands after 1918 and establish statehood so swiftly without the base of social, economic, and cultural development constructed through organic work. Although nonviolent resistance has been widely used by different generations of Poles against both external occupation and domestic dictatorship, this form of struggle is still awaiting much-deserved recognition of its role in not only defending, but essentially reimagining, the Polish nation.[26]

As it is, pretty much all statist institutions of the revived Polish state were created not in resistance but in collaboration with occupying powers. Galician experience of self-government, especially, with a fully Polish-staffed and organized bureaucracy, which lasted a good half a century, was an incomparable preparation for governing an independent state for the Poles, and Galician practices, rules, and bureaucrats spread all over the post-1918 Polish state, exercising an outsized influence on the newly independent Poland. Likewise, the spectrum of legal political parties and the norms and practices of parliamentary life that came from Galicia were responsible for the creation of Polish postindependence political culture as a liberal and democratic parliamentary republic. Little of these beneficial cultural, structural, and institutional legacy had much to do with any form of "national nonviolent resistance": these institutions developed through "normal" political channels and in collaboration with Austria, as I have amply documented here, but a lot of it had to do with nonviolent struggles of Polish lower classes for emancipation from class oppression by their Polish masters—not any type of "national," but rather, class resistance.

In the Russian partition, institutions of the Polish autonomous state were recreated by the German occupiers and simply needed to assert their fully sovereignty with the crumbling of the German power. Again, this had preciously little to do with "nonviolent resistance," as these institutions were mostly created in collaboration with the occupants.

It was only in the German partition of Poland where the existence of fully German bureaucracy and massive oppression of Polishness made the creation of Polish state institutions impossible, and here, the robust civil society created as a part of nonviolent resistance against Germanization had a dramatic role in the creation of postindependence Polish life. Ironically, though, this is also where the most violent episode of the 1918–1919 Polish struggle for independence took place, as the Polish sovereignty over the key part of region was secured through a dramatic and successful violent national uprising against the Germans, deemed to be one of two successful uprisings in the partition's history of Poland[27]

3.4 The Polish case and recovering true national histories

To conclude, the question stands based on this particular case, what conclusion can we draw for Bartkowski's chapter on Polish nonviolent resistance and the literature on nonviolent resistance in general? Clearly, a combination of activist roots and revisionist claims in literature on violent resistance creates historical accounts that are important in their revisionism, but also prone to imprecise conceptualization and weak contextualization of their claims. In the Polish case, phenomena that are not nonviolent resistance are claimed as "nonviolent resistance" (Galicia), while massive episodes of nonviolent resistance are overlooked because they do not fit into narrowly conceived particular definitions. Revisionism also leads to poorly contextualized accounts in which the role of nonviolent resistance in events such as national liberation is overclaimed or simply obfuscated. The role of collaboration with occupying powers in gaining national independence, in turn, is obscured, probably because of activist roots of nonviolence scholarship (the need for "moral purity" of dichotomized accounts: resistance as "good"—collaboration as "bad"). As it was in the Polish case, institutions beneficial to the postindependence state emerged mostly with the permission of or by collaboration with occupiers: illegal institution-building can only go so far. The moralistic accounts also discount the role of historical contingencies and difficult dilemmas of resistance vs. collaboration that they contain. The result is skewed, distorted, and overly moralistic accounts of events that present a picture of the real struggle for independence as too simplified to serve as a blueprint or model for real social struggles.

Let me, finally, draw broader lessons of the Polish struggle for independence and the role of nonviolent resistance in that struggle:

1   Collaboration with occupying powers is often crucial in preserving the substance of national life. It also allows for decisive tactical flexibility in moments when historical contingency suddenly allows for the creation of independent statehood. Holding on to "moral purity" of resistance, whether violent or nonviolent, is often an obstacle in the preservation of national life or in the actual achievement of independence.
2   In retrospect, the multiplicity and even bitter divisions of various factions struggling for independence all serve the national cause, as their pluralism of methods and goals covers all possibilities and sides of the conflict, allowing the national movement to take advantage of various opportunities to enlarge the scope of national life.
3   There is no doubt that violent fights for independence are often catastrophic for national life, regardless of the claims that the "spirit of resistance" was somehow preserved through "rivers of blood." At the same time, nonviolent resistance serves a positive, but limited and historically contingent role in these struggles. It is much easier to build institutions of independence legally and in collaboration with occupying powers, not worrying about the moral ambiguity of temporary collaboration.
4   In later national memory, violent or nonviolent resistance episodes are both preserved, but, like all memories, there are subject to politically defined manipulation in function of current power struggles. There is no broader deterministic logic that necessarily marginalizes nonviolent resistance in favor of violent resistance in national memories.

Current ongoing struggles of national liberation, such the Kurdish and Palestinian ones, both exemplify and should take heed of these four principles.

Notes

1. M. Bartkowski, "Recovering nonviolent history," in *Recovering nonviolent history: Civil resistance in liberation struggles* (Boulder, CO: Lynne Rienner Publishers, 2013a), 1–30.
2. M. Bartkowski, "Forging the Polish nation nonviolently," in *Recovering nonviolent history: Civil resistance in liberation struggles* (Boulder, CO: Lynne-Rienner Publishers, 2013b), 259–278.
3. J. Wojtasik, *Idea walki zbrojnej of niepodległość Polski, 1864–1907* (Wydawnictwo: Ministerstwa Obrony Narodowej, 1987).
4. Stanislaw Kalabiński and F. Tych, *Czwarte powstanie czy pierwsza rewolucja. Lata 1905–1907 na ziemiach polskich* (Warszawa: Wiedza Powszechna, 1969); Adam Podkański, *Odrodzenie czynu niepodleglosciowego przez PPS w okresie rewolucji 1905 roku* (Warszawa: Wydawnictwo DiG, 2008).
5. *Walka zbrojna o niepodległość Polski 1905–1918*, Warszawa Volumen; Wacława Milewska, Janusz Tadeusz Nowak, and M. Zientara, *Legiony polskie 1914–1918, Zarys historii militarnej i politycznej* (Kraków: Ksiegarnia Akademicka, 1998).
6. R. Świątek, "Józefa Piłsudskiego współpraca z wywiadem Austro-Węgier (1909–1915)," *Przegląd historyczny* 84, no. 2 (1993): 165–184.
7. J. Piłsudski, "Zadania praktyczne rewolucji w zaborze rosyjskim," in Wacław Lipiński (ed.), *Pisma zbiorowe* (Warszawa: Instytut Józefa Piłsudskiego, 1910 [1937]), 5–22.
8. The fact that this pro-Russian loyalist is celebrated as a patriotic hero and definitely not marginalized in the dominant narrative of Polish national history is also partially a counter to Bartkowski's notion that episodes of violent resistance are celebrated in Polish institutionalized national memory at the expense of nonviolent activities. More about it follows.
9. Bartkowski, "Recovering nonviolent history," 4–5.
10. E. Chenoweth, "Understanding nonviolent resistance: An introduction," *Journal of Peace Research*, 50, no. 3 (2013): 271.
11. See Mażewski Lech, *Oblany egzamin z polityki. O narodzinach, instnieniu i upadku panstwa polskiego w latach 1806–1874* (Warszawa: Von Borowiecky, 2016), chapter 17.
12. J. Buszko, *Galicja. Polski Piemont?* (Warszawa: Krajowa Agencja Wydawnicza, 1989).
13. See J. Buszko, *Kultura polityczna Galicji* (Kraków: Wydawnictwo Uniwersytetu Jagiellońskiego, 1974); Kazimierz Sowa, *Galicja jako fenomen historyczny i socjologiczny* (Kraków, unpublished manuscript, 1997); J. Lubecki and Andrew Drummond, "Reconstructing Galicia: Mapping the cultural and civic traditions of the former Austrian Galicia in Poland and Ukraine," *Europe-Asia Studies* 62, no. 8 (2010): 1311–1338.
14. J. Buszko, *Dzieje ruchu robotniczego w Galicji Zachodniej (1848–1918)* (Kraków: Wydawnictwo Literackie, 1986).
15. Buszko, *Dzieje ruchu robotniczego*.
16. J. Potoczny, *Od alfabetyzacji do popularyzacji wiedzy. Ruch oswiatowy doroslych w Galicji (1867–1918)* (Rzeszów: Wydawnictwo Wyższej Szkoły Pedagogicznej w Rzeszowie, 1993).
17. Bartkowski mistakenly defines it as "the struggle for land and minds" (Bartkowski, 2013b, p. 266), confusing this specific phenomenon with

overall Germanization efforts in the Polish territories of the German partition. See M. B. Gross, *The war against Catholicism: Liberalism and the Anti-Catholic imagination in nineteenth-century Germany* (Ann Arbor, MI: University of Michigan Press, 2005).
18 See, L. Trzeciakowski, *The Kulturkampf in Prussian Poland*, East European Monographs, no. 223 (New York City: Columbia University Press, 1990).
19 This 1886 very popular novel has been compulsory reading in Polish schools, and I have read it in grade school. It describes one Polish peasant's family struggle to resist German encroachment on their land.
20 Diana Błońska, "Wóz Michała Drzymały. Historia narodowej pamiątki," *Kwartalnik Historii kultury Materialnej* 67 (2019): 275–285.
21 Among others, the job of the Polish Western Institute created in 1944 was to document and study "Polish eternal antagonism against Germany." See Gregor Thum, *Uprooted. How Breslau became Wrocław during century of expulsion* (Princeton: Princeton University Press, 2003), 196.
22 J. Żarnowski, "Z dziejów strajku szkolnego 1905," *Przegląd historyczny* 46, no. 1–2 (1955): 184–212.
23 See. J. Kauffman, *Elusive alliance. The German occupation of Poland in World War I* (Oxford: Harvard University Press, 2015).
24 A. Achmatowiczx, "Akty rosyjskie z marca 1917 roku dotyczące Polski," *Studia z dziejów ZSRR i Europy Środkowej* 22 (2019): 50–93.
25 J. Lubecki, "Poland and the Russian revolution of 1917," in *Global impact of Russia's great war and revolution. Book 1: The arc of revolution 1917–24* (Bloomington, IN: Slavica, 2019), 313–341.
26 Bartkowski, "Forging the Polish nation nonviolently," 259–278.
27 The other one being a successful expulsion of Prussian troops from the same area in 1806 in advance of Napoleon's victorious army. See Antoni Czubiński, *Powstanie Wielkopolskie 1918–1919. Geneza-charakter-znaczenie* (Poznań: Wydawnictwo Kurpisz, 2002 [1978]).

References

Achmatowicz, A. (1987). Akty rosyjskie z marca 1917 roku dotyczące Polski. *Studia z dziejów ZSRR i Europy Środkowej, 22*, 50–93.
Bartkowski, M. (2013a). Recovering nonviolent history. In *Recovering nonviolent history: Civil resistance in liberation struggles* (pp. 1–30). Lynne Rienner Publishers.
Bartkowski, M. (2013b). Forging the polish nation nonviolently. In *Recovering nonviolent history: Civil resistance in liberation struggles* (pp. 259–278). Lynne Rienner Publishers.
Błońska, D. (2019). Wóz Michała Drzymały. Historia narodowej pamiątki. *Kwartalnik Historii kultury Materialnej, 67*(2), 275–285.
Buszko, J. (1974). *Kultura polityczna Galicji*. Wydwanictwo Uniwersytetu Jagiellońskigo.
Buszko, J. (1986). *Dzieje ruchu robotniczego w Galicji Zachodniej (1848–1918)*. Wydawnictwo Literackie.
Buszko, J. (1989). *Galicja. Polski Piemont?* Krajowa Agencja Wydawnicza.

Buszko, J. (1994). Galicyjskie Dziedzictwo II Rzeczypospolitej. In J. Buszko & K. Sowa (Eds.), *Galicja i jej dziedzictwo. Historia i polityka* (Vol. 1, pp. 187–199). Wydawnictwo Wyższej Szkoły Pedagogicznej w Rzeszowie.

Chenoweth, E. (2013). Understanding nonviolent resistance: An introduction. *Journal of Peace Research, 50*(3), 271–276.

Czubiński, A. (2002). *Powstanie Wielkopolskie 1918–1919. Geneza-charakter-znaczenie*. Wydawnictwo Kurpisz.

Gross, M. B. (2005). *The war against Catholicism: Liberalism and the anti-Catholic imagination in nineteenth-century Germany*. University of Michigan Press.

Kalabiński, S., & Tych, F. (1969). *Czwarte Powstanie czy pierwsza Rewolucja. Lata 1905–1907 na ziemiach polskich*. Wiedza Powszechna,

Kauffman, J. (2015). *Elusive alliance. The German occupation of Poland in World War I*. Harvard University Press.

Lipiński, J. (1990). *Walka zbrojna o niepodległość Polski 1905–1918*. Warszawa Volumen.

Lubecki, J. (2019). Poland and the Russian revolution of 1917. In A. Marshall, J. W. Steinberg, & S. Sabol (Eds.), *Global impact of Russia's great war and revolution. Book 1: The arc of revolution 1917–1924* (pp. 313–341). Slavica Publishers.

Lubecki, J., & Drummond, A. (2010). Reconstructing Galicia: Mapping the cultural and civic traditions of the former Austrian Galicia in Poland and Ukraine. *Europe-Asia Studies, 62*(8), 1311–1338.

Martin, B. (2005). Researching nonviolent action: past themes and future possibilities. *Peace and Change, 30*(2), 247–270.

Mażewski, L. (2016). *Oblany egzamin z polityki. O narodzinach, instnieniu i upadku panstwa polskiego w latach 1806–1874*. Von Borowiecky.

Milewska, W., Nowak, T. J., & Zientara, M. (1998). *Legiony polskie 1914–1918. Zarys historii militarnej i politycznej*. Ksiegarnia Akademicka.

Piłsudski, J. (1937). Zadania pratyczne rewolucji w zaborze rosyjskim. In W. Lipiński (Ed.), *Pisma zbiorowe* (pp. 5–22). Instytut Józefa Piłsudskiego.

Podkański, A. (2008). *Odrodzenie czynu niepodleglosciowego przez PPS w okresie rewolucji 1905 roku*. Wydawnictwo DiG.

Potoczny, J. (1993). *Od alfabetyzacji do popularyzacji wiedzy. Ruch oswiatowy doroslych w Galicji (1867–1918)*. Wydawnictwo Wyższej Szkoły Pedagogicznej w Rzeszowie.

Sowa, K. (1997). *Galicja jako fenomen historyczny i sociologiczny* [unpublished manuscript]. Kraków.

Świątek, R. (1993). Józefa Piłsudskiego współpraca z wywiadem Austro-Węgier (1909–1915). *Przegląd historyczny, 84*(2), 165–184.

Thum, G. (2003). *Uprooted. How Breslau became Wrocław during century of expulsion*. Princeton University Press.

Trzeciakowski, L. (1990). *The Kulturkampf in Prussian Poland*. East European Monographs, no. 223. Columbia University Press.

Wojtasik, J. (1987). *Idea walki zbrojnej of niepodległość Polski, 1864–1907*. Wydawnictwo Ministerstwa Obrony Narodowej,

Żarnowski, J. (1955). Z dziejów strajku szkolnego 1905. *Przegląd Historyczny, 46*(1–2), 184–212.

Appendix A

Literature on nonviolent resistance

The scholarship exploded in the wake of the "color revolutions" and the Arab Spring. Bartkowski's edited volume (2013) and Chenoweth's edited special issue of *Journal of Peace Studies* (2013) are paradigmatic of the flood of work, which today counts multiple monographs and articles and has been institutionalized in organizations such as the International Center for Nonviolent Conflict. Prior to that, the literature on nonviolent resistance was steeped in activism and was embodied in works such as Gene Sharpe, *The Politics of Nonviolent Action* (1973). A good review of this older literature is presented by Martin (2005). Newer literature is well summarized by Chenoweth, Perkoski, and Kang (2017). The newest, empirical, turn of research in the field is well exemplified by Bethke and Pinckney (2019).

Appendix B

1907–1914 military planning

Austrians and Germans started planning to use a potential Polish anti-Russian insurrection in the event of a war with Russia as early as the 1870s and 1880s. World War I and the use of internal subversion to destroy Russia, which proved to be a spectacularly successful strategy for the Central Powers in 1917, was thus long in coming and planning. See Wojtasik (1987, chapter 1). Otherwise, see Lipiński (1990).

Appendix C

Key passage from the preface in *Recovering nonviolent history* (2013)

Thus, far from decontextualizing nonviolent forms of contention from violent resistance, this book offers a more nuanced and realistic perspective on nationalist movements and liberation struggles. These movements and struggles relied on an impressive repertoire of civil resistance campaigns that were sometimes interspersed temporally or spatially with violence but, in other cases, were in competition with or opposed to armed insurrection. The point of these histories is not to suggest that the countries could not have gained independence without nonviolent struggle or that civil resistance alone was responsible. Rather, independence came as soon as it did—and often the societies and nascent civic and state institutions had been developed and thus were better prepared for independence—partly because of reliance on civil resistance, which had a profound effect on nation and state building.

(Bartkowski, 2013a, p. 19)

Appendix D

Words from Michal Bobrzyński

Michal Bobrzyński was one of the leaders of the uprising against Russia in 1863. His specific words are as follows:

> By launching the uprising which are preparing, we are fulfilling a (patriotic jl) duty, convinced that to put down the uprising Russia will not only destroy the country, but also will be forced to spill rivers of Polish blood, and this blood will become for years to come an obstacle to any compromise with invaders of our country. We do not presume that even in a half a century our nation will forgive and forget the rivers filled with Polish blood by the enemy.
>
> (Mażewski, 2016, p. 260)

Appendix E

Drzymała's wagon

Michał Drzymała was a Polish peasant in German-occupied areas. German law forbade him to build a house on his own land, but between 1904 and 1909, he used a mobile circus wagon as a dwelling, which, being moved every 24 hours, did not qualify as a permanent house. He thus exploited a loophole in the German law—by the way, this also means that German state, being a Rechsstadt (state of laws), respected its own laws. As Polish historians comment, in the Russian partition, the police would have burned the wagon and arrested Drzymała, law or no law. Drzymała's wagon has been amply memorialized and celebrated. After his death in 1937, the village where he lived was renamed after him (Drzymałowo), and every Polish child learns about Drzymała's wagon. A replica of his wagon stands today in Drzymałowo, while one of his two authentic wagons was on display in various Polish museums during the 1920–1939 period (Błońska, 2019).

Appendix F

Maria Konopnicka's poem, "Rota" or "The oath"

The poem was written in 1908, and its opening, best-known lines go as follows:

> We won't forsake the land we came from,
> We won't let our speech be buried.
> We are the Polish nation, the Polish people,
> From the royal line of Piast.
> We won't let the enemy oppress us.
> So help us God!
> So help us God!
> (. . .)

Then, it goes on in telling lines:

> The German won't spit in our face,
> Nor Germanise our children,
> Our host will arise in arms,
> The Spirit will lead the way.
> We will arise when the golden horn sounds.

After 1918 the song was considered to become the national anthem of Poland and lost, by a tad, against "Dąbrowski's March" in 1927. Bartkowski uses the text of "Dąbrowski's March" to emphasize how the Poles privileged violent struggle for independence in historical memory, seemingly unaware that a song celebrating nonviolent resistance almost became the Polish national anthem.

Appendix G

"The longest war of modern Europe"

This featured historical series was dedicated to telling the story of Polish nonviolent resistance against Germany between 1815 and 1918. It was produced between 1979 and 1981 and aired in 1982, at the peak of Jaruzelski's martial law. The fact that the communist government celebrated Polish nonviolent resistance against Germanization while waging a repressive campaign against Solidarity's nonviolent resistance against Polish communism might appear bizarre, but actually made perfect sense in the tangled games of Polish history and communist legitimacy.

Appendix H

A personal note from the author

On a personal note, my mother was born in Września, the most famous site of the children's and parents' school strike against Germanization. I was therefore brought up on stories of Polish nonviolent resistance against Germanization, and I find the notion that these are somehow marginalized Polish national memory absurd. Pictures of the large concrete monument to Września's children, which shows nine of them can be found here:

https://pl.wikipedia.org/wiki/Pomnik_Dzieci_Wrzesi%C5%84skich_we_Wrze%C5%9Bni.

Appendix I

Polish communism

Poland became communist as a result of Soviet defeat of Germany, and this crushing of the German power and subjugation of Germany within the context of the Soviet-Polish alliance became the source of the Polish communist government's nationalistic legitimacy. Conversely, all Polish anti-communist and democratic opposition, could be labeled by the communists as serving the cause of German revisionism and revanchism. The role that this source of legitimacy played for Polish communist regime cannot be overestimated. This was probably more important than the flimsy ideology of Marxism-Leninism to justify the Polish communist government.

4 Kurdish identity, resistance, and agenda-setting in a time of renewed Turkish hostility
Social media and the HDP

Ned Rinalducci

4.1 Introduction

The land referred to as Kurdistan includes the mountainous region that covers the Zagros mountains and the area where Turkey, Iran, Iraq, and Syria intersect. It is divided between these states and is home to a people who consider themselves to be a distinct ethnic group, not Turkish, Persian, or Arab. The Kurds are the fourth largest group in the Middle East and the world's largest ethnic group without a state of their own.[1] Kurdish nationalism dates back to the late 19th century, around the same time as the "birth" of Arab and Turkish nationalism (McDowall, 2004).[2] In the aftermath of World War I, with the demise of the Ottoman Empire, Kurdish leaders were promised autonomy by the United States, Britain, and France.

> The Treaty of Sevre, signed by the Allies and the Turkish government on August 10, 1920, specifically stipulated that the Kurds were to be allowed "local autonomy." The Treaty . . . was never applied because the subsequent war of independence . . . changed the whole situation and enabled Mustafa Kemal to impose different terms at the Treaty of Lausanne, signed in 1923.[3]

There is an old Kurdish saying, "[W]e have no friends, but the mountains," that is used to express how many times in history Kurds have been on the losing end of international power struggles. With the Treaty of Lausanne, the largest part of Kurdistan became part of the new Turkish Republic, and the Turkish government started a systematic process of Turkification of the Kurdish people, attempting to homogenize the country into one Turkish culture. While Kurdish identity, rights, representation, autonomy, independence, and nationalism have been met with a wide range of outwardly hostile policies throughout all the regions and countries the Kurdish people inhabit,

DOI: 10.4324/9781003109310-4

this study will focus on Turkey and its relationship with its Kurdish population. Turkey is home to more Kurds than any other country, and the history between the Turkish state and Kurdish identity politics has been one defined by discrimination, terrorism, violence, and cultural genocide.

Following the attainment of Turkish independence in 1923, Turkish founding father, Kemal Atatürk, imposed a narrow and ethnic conception of citizenship that privileged the Turkish language and culture and negated Kurdish identity.[4] "The drive to create a unitary, culturally homogenous Turkish state . . . left little room for the free expression of minority cultures and identities."[5] The "Turkification" of the country included exclusionary policies such as denying Kurdish identity, prohibiting use of the Kurdish language—including in radio, television, schools, government, and public places—the renaming of all Kurdish territories with Turkish names, militarizing Kurdish territories, outlawing Kurdish political parties, and banning Kurdish cultural activities.[6] The denial of Kurdish identity went so far as to claim that Kurds were simply "Mountain Turks," who had lost touch with their Turkish identity.[7] Thus, the "Kurdish question" emerged as the outcome of the homogenizing Kemalist nation-building process and the Turkification of all other identities.[8] The new state feared that any identity other than Turkish could present a challenge to the new country's territorial integrity and divide the state.[9]

4.2 The PKK—Kurdistan Workers Party

Decades of Kurdish pressure had wrested little if anything in terms of Kurdish cultural or political rights, despite Kurdish unrest and uprisings dating back to the 1920s and 1930s.[10] It was not until the 1960s that the state discourse on Kurds started being challenged by Kurdish activists, who were often detained and sentenced to jail.[11] But it was the founding of the Kurdistan Workers Party, or the PKK (Partîya Karkerên Kurdistanê), in 1978 that truly started the modern movement for Kurdish rights, Kurdish identity, and Kurdish nationalism in Turkey.[12] The PKK had a nationalist agenda and nonviolence was not part of it. The new organization sought to "take up arms against the Turkish state and launch a war for an independent Kurdistan in Turkey's southeastern region."[13]

The PKK held that state repression meant no alternative avenue of political expression was available other than violence.[14] The period of greatest conflict was from 1984 to the late 1990s, which led to more than 45,000 deaths, including soldiers, guerrillas, and civilians. The southeastern Kurdish regions of Turkey were put under emergency rule or some form of martial law from 1980 until the early 2000s. Approximately, one-third of the entire Turkish military was permanently deployed to the region.[15] The founder and leader of the PKK, Abdullah Öcalan, started the organization with several fellow college students of Kurdish descent in the late 1970s. While they founded it as a Marxist-Leninist Kurdish movement of national liberation, it was not until the 1980s that the organization took up arms. "The massive repression which followed the military coup in 1980 sparked off the PKK's armed struggle, which started in August 1984."[16] Öcalan was considered more than the leader of the movement; he is referred to as Apo, meaning uncle, implying a paternal familial position over the Kurdish community. He remained the leader of the PKK from its founding until his arrest in 1999. With the help of the United States, Turkish authorities arrested Öcalan in Kenya after Syria would no longer offer him protection.[17] Öcalan was sentenced to death after his trial, but the Turkish state has since commuted his sentence to life in prison. Currently, he is imprisoned on Imrali Island, a small prison island in the Sea of Marmara. Since his imprisonment, Öcalan has lobbied for a nonviolent solution to the Kurdish issue and has participated in secret negotiations with the Turkish government from his island prison cell.

The PKK was founded as a revolutionary social organization. In their own literature they describe themselves as "leading a national liberation struggle to free Kurdistan from colonialist and imperialist occupation and carry out a democratic social revolution within Kurdish society."[18] The PKK has been labeled as a terrorist group by many countries around the world, including the United States and the European Union.[19] While founded with a mix of Marxist-Leninist and nationalist ideologies with the goal of establishing an independent Kurdistan, the PKK has moved away from such rigid ideology to embrace a form of democratic confederalism and libertarian socialism with an emphasis on feminism and gender politics. The goal of an independent Kurdish state was replaced with the recognition of Kurdish political, social, and cultural rights within a decentralized Turkey.[20] Öcalan would trade Marx for Murray Bookchin, an American anarchist thinker who favored democratic decentralization and strong local assemblies.[21]

Until the early 1990s, the Turkish state had ruled out any discussion of a peaceful resolution to its Kurdish problem and labeled the issue one of terrorism and security. Turkish president Turgat Ozal changed that in the early 1990s and started a dialogue with the PKK through intermediaries such as Jalal Talabani, head of the Patriotic Union of Kurdistan in Iraq. Unfortunately, his efforts to bring the sides together died with him in 1993.[22] Despite the attempts at multiple PKK ceasefires, no real talk of the Kurdish problem would be part of the public discourse again until the rise of the AKP (Adalet ve Kalkınma Partisi), or the Justice and Development Party, in 2002. The AKP would change Turkey's political landscape.

Kurdish resistance and agenda setting 63

As a conservative party with its roots in Islam, it challenged the strict secular nationalist ideology of Kemalism. This also created an opportunity for dialogue about other political movements that challenged the old Kemalist order, specifically, ethnic identity, and the situation of Kurds in Turkey. Headed by Recep Tayyip Erdoğan, the AKP was founded as "a moderate, social conservative party with Islamic roots in August 2001 after the two previous Islamic parties—the Virtue Party (Fazilet Partisi) and the Welfare Party (Refah Partisi)—had been banned."[23] The AKP regime seemed set on accommodating Kurdish rights and brokering an end to violence with the PKK. Even though it was strongly disapproved of by the old-guard Kemalist nationalists, AKP leaned toward establishing a broader political settlement. But it was not to be. In the end, differing objectives, and the AKP demanding a complete disarming of the PKK before any legal guarantees for Kurdish fighters and leaders would be discussed, led to an impasse.[24] Since the 2015 parliamentary gains of the HDP (Halkların Demokratik Partisi) or the People's Democratic Party, a Kurdish-dominated left-wing party that robbed the AKP of its absolute majority in parliament, Erdoğan has decided military force is now the only solution to the Kurdish problem.[25] In recent years, the tensions and hostilities have not only been renewed, they have crossed national borders.

4.3 The HDP and "Kurdish" political parties

The history of Kurdish-based political parties in Turkey has been a story of the state playing whack-a-mole with each newly formed organization. It is a history of parties starting, being banned, and starting again with new names and sometimes new leadership. Throughout the modern history of Turkey, Kurdish-based political parties formed, only to be banned by the constitutional court over charges ranging from supporting activities that would divide the state to being connected to and supporting terrorism, specifically the PKK. From the People's Labor Party (HEP) to the Peoples' Democratic Party (HDP), the various parties of the "Kurdish Left" (a term used by Celep to describe the modern Kurdish political party movements, 2014)[26] have included the People's Labor Party (HEP) from 1990 to1993, the Freedom and Equality Party (ÖZEP) from 1992 until it merged with the HEP, the Freedom and Democracy Party (ÖZDEP) from 1992 to 1993, the Democracy Party (DEP) from 1991 to 1994, the People's Democracy Party (HADEP) from 1994 to 2003, the Democratic People's Party (DEHAP) from 1997 until it dissolved to join with DTP, the Democratic Society Party (DTP) from 2005 to 2009, the Peace and Democracy Party (BDP) from 2008 until it merged with HDP in 2014, and the Peoples' Democratic Party (HDP) from 2012 to the present.[27] However, the HDP was the first party of the Kurdish Left to field candidates as a party for parliament, despite the danger of potentially falling below the 10% threshold and losing all representation. Previously, Kurdish politicians would run as independents or in coalitions with, and under, the umbrellas of other left-wing Turkish parties. For example, the pro-Kurdish HEP (Halkin Emek Partisi—People's Labor Party) joined in a coalition with the SHP (Sosyal Demokrat Halkçi Parti—Social Democratic Populist Party) in 1991, making them part of a governing coalition with the DYP (Doğru Yol Partisi—True Path Party), until opposing forces in the parliament, military, and judiciary stripped all Kurdish deputies of their positions and arrested and imprisoned them.[28] Table 4.1 documents the transitions and changes in the Kurdish Left parties from the creation of the HEP in 1990 to the current HDP. Table 4.1 lists the history of Kurdish political parties with the dates each party started and ended from 1990 to the present.

As a result of the 2017 Turkish constitutional referendum, the number of the seats in the parliament was raised from 550 to 600. There is now a presidential system in place, giving the president executive powers and doing away with the position of prime minister.

Table 4.1 From HEP to HDP

Party title	Date opened	Date closed
People's Labor Party (HEP)	June 7, 1990	July 14, 1993
Freedom and Equality Party (ÖZEP)	June 25, 1992	Merged HEP
Freedom and Democracy Party (ÖZDEP)	October 19, 1992	November 23, 1993
Democracy Party (DEP)	June 21, 1991	June 16, 1994
People's Democracy Party (HADEP)	May 11, 1994	March 13, 2003
Democratic People's Party (DEHAP)	October 24, 1997	November 19, 2005*
Democratic Society Party (DTP)	November 9, 2005	December 11, 2009
Peace and Democracy Party (BDP)	May 2, 2008	April 22, 2014**
Democratic Regions Party (DBP)	May 2, 2008	-
Peoples' Democratic Party (HDP)	October 15, 2012	-

Source: Celep, Ö. (2014). Can the Kurdish Left contribute to Turkey's democratization? *Insight 16*(3), 171.

* Dissolved itself to join DTP.
**Dissolved itself to join DBP and HDP separately.

The Turkish parliamentary system is set up to favor larger parties. As of 2017, the Grand National Assembly has 600 seats. A party needs 10% of the vote to get seated in parliament with any representation. The 10% threshold is quite high when compared to similar systems in Germany (5%), Sweden (4%), or Denmark (2%). Theoretically, if a party were to win 40 seats, but only receive 9.55% of the national vote, they forfeit all their seats, which are then reallocated to those parties who did meet the threshold.[29] The HDP, the Peoples' Democratic Party, became the first pro-Kurdish party to cross the 10% threshold required to enter the Turkish parliament in the election of June 7, 2015.[30]

Of particular interest is the way the HDP positioned and shaped itself into a popular party with concerns that go beyond Kurdish rights. The party, in its efforts to move beyond its Kurdish base, represents itself as more than a party of Kurdish interests. It became an umbrella party of disparate interests including human rights, feminism, and gender equality, LGBTQ rights, environmentalism, workers' rights, rights of non-Muslim minorities, and rights for Alevis, Yazidis, Syriacs, the Roma, Armenians, and Circassians. Their platform includes support for scientific and secular education in mother tongues, opposition to compulsory religious education, the closure of juvenile prisons, the legal recognition of the right to conscientious objection, and favors a democratized parliamentary system over the presidential system supported by Erdoğan and the AKP.[31] The Turkish word *çokrenklilik* is used to describe the multiple "colors" of the party. As then HDP leader Selahattin Demirtaş stated: "Turkey without the HDP would be grey only."[32] One supporter explained it as no longer being a Kurdish party, but a Kurdish-dominated party.[33] Selahattin Demirtaş, one of the early cochairs of the HDP, has been dubbed the "Kurdish Obama" for his good looks and dynamic speaking style as well as his statesmanship.[34] Demirtaş shared the chair position with Figen Yüksekdağ, as the HDP's gender inclusive structure mandates two chairs, one male and one female, and was also a candidate for president in the 2018 presidential election, coming in third.

It is believed that this transformation into a Turkish party advocating for Kurdish rights among other policy priorities is what helped lift the party past the 10% threshold.[35] The Kurdish political movement came to represent more than exclusively Kurdish politics and positioned itself as a vehicle for multiculturalism and democracy. The HDP's vision of a Turkey that is *"hem çok renkli hem çok dilli"* (both multicolored and multilingual) and encompasses not only Kurds but a variety of other religious, ethnic, and oppressed groups stands in marked contrast to the increasingly nationalistic and authoritarian AKP regime.[36] The HDP remains the third largest party in the 600-seat Grand National Assembly.

4.4 Election aftermath and attempted coup

The already antagonistic relationship between Erdoğan and the HDP took another turn for the worse in July of 2016 when an attempted coup against Erdoğan and his AKP government was thwarted. Turkey has a history of military coups (e.g., 1960, 1980, along with military interventions in 1971 and 1997), and the coup plotters, most likely Gülenists, believed they could take advantage of that tradition. Erdoğan termed the failed coup and its aftermath a "gift from God," giving him an excuse to go after all his political rivals and enemies. All the Turkish party leaders, including the HDP cochairs, condemned the coup. Erdoğan, in an expression of thanks, invited all the party leaders except Demirtaş and Yüksekdağ to the presidential palace. Erdoğan did this to politically isolate the HDP and was a sign of things to come.[37] In the days and weeks following the coup attempt, purges of state institutions and a series of show trials were enacted to further consolidate Erdoğan's power.[38] As for the HDP, their condemnation of the coup did not shield them from Erdoğan's wrath. In the aftermath of the attempt, HDP leaders Selahattin Demirtaş and Figen Yüksekdağ were detained, along with other HDP MPs, over their refusal to testify about sham crimes linked to "terrorist propaganda."[39] Erdoğan successfully stripped Demirtaş and other HDP MPs of their parliamentary immunity, allowing him to wrongfully prosecute them for treason.[40]

Before the attempted coup, Erdoğan was already alienating those friendly to the Kurdish cause, as can be seen in the prosecution of "Academics for Peace," a group of initially 1,128 academics who signed a petition critical of Turkey's renewed violence in the southeast (Human Rights Watch, 2017).[41] Erdoğan purposefully targeted the Kurdish cause as a means to rally nationalist support to his party. Kurdish and other opposition media were shut down, including *Ozgur Gundem*, a pro-Kurdish newspaper, and IMC TV, a television network known for its pro-Kurdish and liberal content. Erdoğan blamed his former ally Fethullah Gülen, and the Gülenist movement—a socially and politically active Islamic group—for the failed coup attempt. He would go on to make preposterous claims that Gülen was working with "Armenian Brigands," the Kurdish PKK, and YPG as part of a "treason gang." Despite the fact that there has never been any evidence for such claims, they, nonetheless, became a fundamental part of Erdoğan's narrative about the coup.[42] Under the pretext of supporting terrorism, leaders of the HDP were arrested as part of the post-coup crackdown. Authorities claimed they were targeting anyone with links to Fethullah Gülen and the PKK, despite their differing ideologies and the lack of any evidence linking them to one another.

Although the AKP dominated the 2019 local elections, HDP still did well in the majority-Kurdish east of the country.[43] In March 2019, HDP mayoral candidates won 65 Turkish municipalities, only to have Erdoğan take control of all but ten of those. As of February 2020, 32 HDP mayors had been removed from office and replaced with provincial and district governor "trustees."[44] The most common rationale for these actions is the claim that the mayors support the PKK and terrorism. Despite all the negative developments, the HDP still stands as a party and recently completed its party congress in Ankara. Once again, the HDP was able to surpass the required 10% threshold in the parliamentary elections of 2018 and continues to be a significant political actor in Turkey's politics. In December 2020, the European Court of Human Rights ruled that Turkey must release HDP leader Selahattin Demirtaş, finding the justification for his imprisonment was a cover for limiting pluralism and debate.[45]

4.5 Outside factors—EU and Syria

Any discussion of the current Kurdish situation in Turkey must take into account two external factors that had both positive and negative effects on the Kurdish movement: Turkey's one-time desire to enter into the European Union and the civil war in Syria. Early in the AKP/Erdoğan era, Turkey's acceptance as an EU candidate country in 1999 played a significant role in how Turkey would move forward with the Kurdish question.[46] This period of the Erdoğan regime witnessed the drafting of legislation to eliminate torture, expand freedom of expression and association, restore Kurdish names to Kurdish villages, and enable Kurdish language broadcasting by public and private radio and television stations. Amnesty laws were discussed, and Kurdish language departments in universities were allowed to operate in Kurdish-majority cities.[47] It was a productive and promising time in the history of Turkish-Kurdish relations, as EU membership would bring Turkey closer to European norms of pluralistic inclusive democracies, but it was not to last. Erdoğan would eventually give up on the idea of EU membership and look east instead of west.

The second major development affecting the Turkish-Kurdish question had to do with the situation of Kurds in neighboring countries. In Iraq, the Kurdistan Regional Government (KRG) rules northern Iraq with great autonomy from the national government. There are fears that if the KRG achieves independence, it will give rise to a similar movement in Turkey. While the 2017 referendum on independence passed in the KRG region with overwhelming support, ultimately, pressure from Turkey, the United States, and the international community prevented the KRG from officially declaring that independence.

The situation in Syria is similar, but closer to home for Turkey. In Iraq, the Turkish government has a working relationship with the KRG, while in Syria, the Turkish government associates the primary Kurdish organizations—the PYD (Democratic Union Party) and YPG (Peoples Protection Units)—as too connected to the Turkish PKK. The PYD is sometimes referred to as the Syrian branch of the PKK. Once the civil war in Syria started in 2011, the Kurdish PYD/YPG would eventually become a major player among the disparate groups vying for power. The Kurdish forces would eventually work with the United States in the war against Islamic State (ISIS/ISIL) by establishing the Syrian Democratic Forces (SDF), an umbrella group for Syrian militias dominated by the YPG. As the war against ISIS saw SDF victories, large swaths of Syrian territory came under the control of Kurdish forces. The Syrian Kurds named these territories Rojava and attempted to govern them according to their progressive democratic values. The Turkish government found this unacceptable. Erdoğan and the HDP perceive a second autonomous Kurdish region on Turkey's border as a direct threat to Turkish territorial integrity. The formation of Rojava, along with the HDP electoral success of 2015, is the primary basis for renewed animosity against the Turkish Kurds.

Erdoğan so feared what Rojava stood for that he was accused of favoring ISIS in the battle for control of Syria. Turkey's do-nothing policy concerning the battle for Kobane on the Turkish border between Kurdish and ISIS forces from September 2014 to January 2015 is evidence of this fear. As Erdoğan saw it, support for the Syrian Kurds in Kobane would be nothing short of aiding the terrorists. In fact, as long as the Kurds and ISIS were fighting each other, Turkey benefited.[48] ISIS was seen as a tool to combat the PKK/ PYD/YPG/Rojava and a means to help bring down the Syrian regime.[49] An ISIS fighter is recorded saying that ISIS had nothing to fear from Turkey, because they shared a common enemy.[50] The territorial gains of Kurds in Syria pushed Erdoğan toward a more extreme nationalistic and aggressive position, vis-à-vis the Kurds in Turkey. As a result, he adopted a much tougher posture toward the PKK and the Kurdish movement.[51] The idea of autonomous Kurdish regions in both Syria and Iraq, which would leave Turkey bordering a greater Kurdistan, was more than Erdoğan could take. "We will never allow the establishment of a state on our southern border in the north of Syria. . . . We will continue our fight in that respect whatever the cost may be," said Erdoğan.[52] Both these outside factors are important in understanding the position of the Kurdish movement inside Turkey, especially the events in Syria occurring simultaneously with the perceived political threats from the HDP.

4.6 Human rights issues and testimony

The international human rights movement is generally described as being launched toward the beginning of the 20th century with the drafting and eventual adoption of the Universal Declaration of Human Rights (UDHR) in 1948.[53] Turkey was among the member nations that adopted the UDHR, which can be found on the official Republic of Turkey Ministry for Foreign Affairs website,[54] and in 1954 the European Convention of Human Rights put Turkey under the jurisdiction of the European Court of Human Rights. While some scholars claim that the ideals in the UDHR are Eurocentric, marginalizing the values of other peoples and imposing a form of cultural imperialism on the non-Western world,[55] others have pointed out that the UDHR was drafted by a committee of diverse world leaders, including Charles Malik from Lebanon; Peng-chun Chang from China; and Hernán Santa Cruz from Chile under the influence of Bertha Lutz, a Brazilian biologist, feminist, and lawyer, and Hansa Mehta, an Indian delegate and activist.[56]

Since the midcentury, the language of human rights has increasingly become the common language of social criticism in global political life.[57] This is particularly true in Turkey, where since the 1980s, the "language of human rights" became the "only available means of dissent," the only viable way to organize a resistance to the government. At that time, the government was led by the military, which persecuted all perceived political enemies.[58] While times and ruling parties change, the Turkish IHD (Human Rights Association), an NGO first formed in the 1980s, continued to be a safe space for those who wished to engage in any political struggle outside of the mainstream until the mid-1990s. While joining associations other than the approved political parties was illegal, IHD's focus on human rights allowed it to occupy a special space in public life. When the AKP, led by Erdoğan, seemed to support an expansion of human rights in Turkey, a number of additional human rights organizations and associations quickly proliferated. While the days of Westernized "progress" toward a society that honored and protected human rights did not last,[59] the fact that Turkey had been fighting for such rights before the AKP began its failed attempt to join the EU, combined with the continued existence of a wide variety of diverse, relatively autonomous civil organizations for human rights has meant that the human rights movement in Turkey continues to struggle for justice and to serve as a platform of political opposition.[60]

Sharing the testimonial narratives of victims of human rights violations is a central element of human rights work throughout the world. In Turkey, for example, the IHD was formed by lawyers and women who were victims of such violations and who saw their role in the organization as activists who must give voice to the atrocities they had suffered.[61] In the academic world as well, collecting such narratives "has become the dominant approach for social scientists addressing the aftermath of violence."[62] While there is certainly a danger of imposing a narrative structure on human suffering that reproduces conventional knowledge rather than honors authentic experience, it is impossible to deny the power of such narratives in the social and political realm. The multiple voices and perspectives found on Twitter, packaged in short bursts of 240 characters, rarely creates a cohesive narrative structure in transmission. Yet we believe that like traditional narratives of victims of crimes against humanity, the messages of human rights activists on Twitter can bring to light events and abuses that otherwise the world would never see.

4.7 Technology and resistance

This study examines what issues the HDP, as the primary pro-Kurdish political party in Turkey, highlights when communicating to English-speaking audiences on social media in light of the oppressive policies and human rights violations of the Edroğan/AKP regime. Even while under state attack, they are consistent in their nonviolent democratic inclusiveness, as they remain the legal voice of Kurdish politics in Turkey. As the HDP has been "effectively blacklisted from [traditional] Turkish media,"[63] social media and communication from platforms such as Twitter and Facebook, have become all the more important. Social media use in Turkey is high; penetration of leading social media networks puts Twitter at 61%, Facebook at 76%, and even higher for YouTube, Instagram, and WhatsApp.[64] For this reason, Turkey is passing new social media laws to limit their influence.[65]

While political messaging takes place on many social media platforms, Twitter and Facebook are the most influential of these platforms, as measured by the number of users around the world and the frequency of political messaging and advertising on those platforms. Research finds that Facebook is more popular with local candidates and campaigns, while Twitter is generally the preferred platform for national and global political actors.[66] This is in part due to the nature of each platform. Facebook requires users to register using their real identity and is designed to facilitate lengthy private and semi-private communication between "friends." Twitter, on the other hand, is primarily a public platform that allows for anonymity and is designed to provide a platform for users to share short, timely messages to their "followers." Such anonymity, to the extent that it can be maintained, can be particularly conducive to resistance.

Social media has become an important and effective element of political outreach and mobilization.[67] While traditional forms of mass media rely upon a member of the press—a journalist, news anchor, editor, and so on—to transmit information to audiences, social media allows political actors to communicate directly with audiences, filter-free. A systematic review of research studying the use of Twitter in election campaigns[68] found that parties and candidates use Twitter to share information about their campaign events and activities more often than they post about policy issues or make explicit calls for action. Thus, the potential for social media to become a conduit for direct interaction between political actors and audiences has not yet been realized on a grand scale, although scholars are beginning to suggest that former US president Trump used the medium to effectively reach his political base.[69]

A growing body of research seeking to understand when, why, and how (or *if*) political actors are able to influence audiences on social media has emerged over the last two decades. While Dimitrova and Mattes[70] posit that social scientific research related to social media and political messaging around the world "lacks overarching theoretical frameworks or models, ideally competing ones, which can guide our selection of concepts and help to contextualize our findings," many researchers are applying tried-and-true theoretical perspectives to what is a relatively new phenomenon.

4.8 Agenda-setting, agenda-building, and the two-step flow model

The explanatory power of agenda-setting theory,[71] and the two-step flow of communication model,[72] while rooted in the days of print and radio, have continued to be applicable to technologies not imagined nearly a century ago. The agenda-setting function of media as a theoretical concept refers to how news media influence what the public believes are the most important social and political issues of the day. The particular stories the news media choose to report, along with the frequency of publishing those stories, increases the salience of those issues, ultimately impacting the public agenda.[73] When agenda-setting, the news media does not prescribe a particular cause, solution, or value judgment related to an issue, but instead ensures that the issue becomes an important part of the broader political and public agenda. As Cohen famously said, "The press may not be successful much of the time in telling people what to think, but it is stunningly successful in telling its readers what to think *about*."[74]

While theorizing about agenda-setting began as a means of understanding the impact of print news on political campaigns, it has since expanded into a wide subset of interrelated theories and is applied to all types of media and political speech.[75] The theoretical focus of this study is on agenda-setting as it relates to issue salience and agenda-building. Media agenda-building refers to the efforts of political actors, such as candidates, elected officials, political parties, or political interest groups, to influence agenda-setting in the media.[76] Press releases, videos, speeches, and social media are all considered "information subsidies" designed to impact the mass media agenda. Research on the impact of social media as agenda-building finds that journalists rely heavily on Twitter to inform their reporting,[77] confirming that agenda-building has a meaningful impact on agenda-setting.[78] However, it is important to note that the relationship between political actors and the media is not unidirectional. Instead, journalists and politicians are mutually dependent on each other in the transmission of information,[79] creating a reciprocal effect in which the media influences the agenda of political actors even as those actors seek to influence the media.[80] It is also of note that journalists indicate tweets from political bloggers, think tanks, and interest groups are more influential to their reporting than tweets from candidates and politicians.[81]

While the media and political actors have a direct influence over each other when agenda-setting, the two-step flow model of communication theorizes how such agendas are transmitted to the public. The "magic bullet" theory of communication suggests that news media influence audiences by transmitting information directly to them—the way a person might shoot a magic bullet directly into someone's head.[82] However, this model is simplistic and fails to take into account network effects. The two-step flow model of communication posits that most people are politically influenced, not directly by the news media, but by opinion leaders within their social network.[83] The two-step flow model continues to find empirical support, even in the digital age when applied to social media effects. When determining if a political agenda influences voting or other political actions, Bene found that the average number of shares from candidates' Facebook pages positively correlated with election outcomes,[84] while the number of likes and comments—both an indication of audience engagement—were not correlated with election outcomes. Analyzing Twitter-based political discussions in South Korea, Choi found that while a small number of opinion leaders were highly influential within their networks, these opinion leaders were not content creators.[85] When studying how Twitter impacted public opinion about the 2016 US presidential election, Alfarhoud found that the majority of opinion leaders were individual users rather than campaigns, organizations, or affiliations.[86]

Because social media is interactive, audiences now have unprecedented access to agenda-setters and agenda-builders. This opens up the possibility that agenda-setting is not a unidirectional activity, but could be to some degree reciprocal. Stier et al. found a disparity between how the general public ranks the importance of specific issues to how politicians rank the importance of these issues, and this was explained by the influence "a specific subset of politically engaged citizens" had on politicians.[87] They conclude that "political communication in general is mediated by varying sociotechnical affordances of social media platforms (p. 73)."[88]

To understand a political actor's agenda, we typically look at how salient certain issues or events are in their messaging, as measured by how frequently these variables appear in the data. Both quantitative and qualitative content analyses of political speech are methods frequently utilized to understand the underlying agenda of news media and political actors. Knowing that audience interaction with social media is most impactful on other users when messages are shared, by looking at "retweets" on Twitter, we can determine which issues resonate most with the portion of an audience that are influencers.

4.9 Research questions, method, and analysis

This study seeks answer to the following questions. (RQ1) What issues does the HDP prioritize in its agenda-building role, as communicated to their English-speaking audiences on Twitter? (RQ2) What issues resonate the most with the influencers within HDPEnglish's audience, as measured by the most frequently retweeted messages? (RQ3) How do these issues differ, if at all, from the overall agenda of HDPEnglish? To answer these questions, we sampled the content of tweets posted to Twitter by the HDP on their English-language Twitter account: HDPEnglish. At the time of sampling, a total of 4,812 tweets had been posted since the account's inception in March 2014, to as many as 21,900 followers. The Twitter API allowed us to download a total of 3,200 of the most recent tweets, dated from June 16, 2015, to December 31, 2020. The data included the full text of the tweets, the language of the tweet, a link to any websites included in the tweets, notation if a photo or video was included in the tweet, the date and time of posting, the number of "favorites" and retweets each tweet received, the user who posted the tweet, and if it was a retweet or a response to another tweet. Although it is an English-language site, a small portion of the tweets were in a wide variety of other languages. Eliminating those left us with a total of 2,987 tweets for analysis.

Newer technologies provide researchers with powerful tools for analyzing large quantities of unstructured data, including social media messages.[89] For the purposes of our inquiry, we have chosen to utilize Provalis Wordstat, a quantitative text mining and content analysis software with similar functioning to RStudio.[90] Wordstat allows for both inductive exploratory research and deductive analysis. After importing the data set, we preprocessed the data to eliminate high-frequency irrelevant words ("a," "an," "the," for example) using a typical English-language stop-word dictionary. In the inductive phase of our study, we began with conducting a frequency word count–based analysis that identified the words and phrases most frequently used in the data. This was done by using the topic-modeling function of the software, which groups clusters of words and phrases based on synonyms, stemming, and proximity.

Following the methodology of other researchers utilizing computer-assisted text mining,[91] we began by identifying the most frequently referenced words and phrases in all tweets, followed by employing exploratory topic modeling using factor analysis. To determine if the identified topics and related word clusters had any meaning, we looked extensively at hundreds of keywords in context, followed by cross-referencing them with records of current events. Eventually, a set of broad organizing categories emerged, representing the most salient concepts found within the data. These categories were actors, events, human rights issues, and rhetorical strategies.

Because content analysis is highly contextual,[92] and because the existing body of predefined text mining dictionaries is still quite limited, it was determined that creating a new dictionary (also known as a *categorization model*) was necessary to analyze the data. Thus, within the four categories, a word list was generated using concepts related to the original articles of United Nations Declaration of Human Rights[93] and subsequent literature on the evolution of human rights movements, both globally and specific to Turkey.[94]

These word lists were grouped into topics and subtopics as appropriate. The keywords are not exclusive, meaning that a word or phrase could be included in more than one category or subcategory. This method of categorization was essential, as a word that might be in one category, such as "events" could quite easily fall into another category, such as "human rights—war crimes," and a forced choice between them would lead to an incomplete and, thus, invalid analysis. However, by allowing words to be included in more than one category, comparisons using word frequency percentages are entirely unreliable. Instead, our analysis focuses on the number of cases (individual tweets) in which keywords are found, as compared to the entire body of tweets, to determine salience.

The completed HDPEnglish Social Media Dictionary allowed us to take a deductive approach to answering our research questions. We determined that data found within the human rights issues category was most applicable to the current project. However, within the actors category, one keyword was so salient, occurring in 1,042 tweets, that we felt it important to include it in our discussion: "Demirtaş." In addition, we looked at keywords related to Kurdish identity, to determine if the notion had a similar degree of salience. Finding the frequencies for all 574 keywords within the human rights issues, organized by topics and subtopics, answered RQ1. To answer RQ2, we identified the top 5% of tweets with the most retweets (N150) and analyzed the data using the same dictionary used to answer RQ1. To answer RQ3, we created a norm file based on the total frequencies of keywords in the entire data set and then used the HDPEnglish Social Media Dictionary to quantify the same keywords in the top 5% of retweets. Then a comparison to the norm file was performed, computing each item's expected frequency, the deviation from the observed frequency, the Z value (standardized deviation) and its two-tailed probability.

Looking at RQ1, we can see that the issues of civil and political rights, as well as human rights violations, make up the majority of topics from the HDPEnglish Twitter page. Together, these two topics make up more than half of all tweets analyzed (1397 and 1097, respectively). Keywords within the civil and political rights category include words related to a fair and impartial judicial system as well as words related to false accusations linking HDP to terrorism for political ends. War crimes and crimes against humanity include keywords used by the United Nations to define such crimes. Diversity/minority rights include keywords related to women's rights, racism, and LGBTQ+ rights. This last category was dominated by issues related to women's rights, with 211 cases, compared to a mere 12 cases for racism and 11 for LGBTQ. Reflecting the topical nature of Twitter, the racism subcategory included two references to the Black Lives Matter movement and a hashtag in one case connecting the Kurdish issue to this movement: #KurdishLivesMatter. Issues related to free speech and state propaganda were relatively low in frequency as well. Human rights general included words and phrases that could clearly be connected to human rights (e.g., human_rights; peace; rights_watch) but did not fall within any other human rights category. Thus, the relatively low frequency of cases does not reflect the overall salience of human rights issues in the data. Economic/social/cultural rights were also fairly low on the frequency distribution. These words were related to workers' rights, speaking the Kurdish language and celebrating holidays and traditions specific to the Kurdish culture. While one might expect this category to rank higher in frequency, because the Kurds in Turkey are facing serious human rights violations related to social and cultural rights, many of the references to these rights fell into the crimes against humanity category instead. In delving more deeply into the subcategories of the human rights categories, we find that war crimes are by far the most salient topic, followed by the judicial/legal category. Democracy and fair elections are also a significant focus of HDP tweets. In fact, these three subcategories make up 76.46% of all human rights subcategories, relegating the remaining nine subcategories to less than one-quarter of all tweets. Therefore, the study concludes that the HDP heavily prioritizes issues related to war crimes, judicial and legal human rights, and democracy in its agenda-building function.

Following RQ2 and RQ3, the analysis shows the frequency of topics found in the top 5% of HDPEnglish retweets (N149), ranged from a low of 97 retweets to a high of 759. We find that the same three topics identified in answering RQ1 are also most salient in this data set: war crimes, judicial and legal human rights, and democracy/fair elections. However, when comparing the top 5% of retweets to the entire data set by computing each item's expected frequency, the deviation from the observed frequency, the Z value (standardized deviation) and its two-tailed probability, some interesting differences do emerge. War crimes/crimes against humanity, judicial/legal rights, and democracy/fair elections categories still represent the three most salient issues within the texts. While these topics represented 76.46% of all the cases in our analysis, for the top retweets, these topics represent 97.3% of all cases. For the war crimes subtopic, the expected frequency of keywords within the tweets is 83.1, but the actual frequency was much higher, at 135 tweets. This represents a highly significant ($p < 0.00$) deviation of 69.7% from the norm. At the other end of the spectrum, issues related to diversity and minority rights (women's rights, LGBTQ+ rights, racism) were significantly underrepresented in the retweets. This category was represented only a third of the expected number of times when looking at frequency ($p < 0.005$). This suggests that the answer to RQ2 is similar to the answer to RQ1, when asking what issues resonate the most with the influencers within HDPEnglish's audience, as measured by the most frequently retweeted messages. We found that influencers among HDPEnglish's followers prioritize issues related to war crimes, judicial and legal human rights, and democracy even more heavily than the HDP, measured by the keywords in HDPEnglish tweets that are most frequently retweeted.

Information about war crimes was significantly more likely to be retweeted than expected, while judicial and legal rights and democracy issues were also somewhat more likely to be retweeted. On the other hand, with the exception of authoritarianism, all tweets related to all other categories in the dictionary were less likely to be retweeted than expected, based on the norm data. This answers RQ3 and suggests that while influencers within HDPEnglish's audience have similar priorities to those demonstrated by the HDP, they are significantly more likely to prioritize issues related to war crimes and less likely to retweet issues related to minority rights. See appendices for tables and figures.

4.10 Discussion

This study looked at how social media can be used to identify the most salient topics the HDP discusses to give us insight into their priorities and their perspective. As mentioned, through both the computer-assisted content analysis of tweets, and human categorization of those findings, it was determined that HDP tweets fall into four broad categories: human rights, events, rhetoric, and people/actors. From a holistic view, these four categories are woven together like threads in a tapestry that illustrate the human suffering, outrage, hope, despair, and resilience experienced by so many of the Kurdish people struggling for basic human rights within the Turkish political machine.

Human rights

The most salient and important category running through HDPEnglish's Twitter feed was human rights. Human rights was constructed to include (1) civil and political rights; (2) war crimes and crimes against humanity; (3) diversity and minority rights; (4) human rights general; and (5) economic, social, and cultural rights. It should not be surprising that human rights, particularly civil and political rights, and war crimes/crimes against humanity are the most frequent. The HDP is experiencing intense legal persecution as of the writing of this study. HDP leaders are being removed from office, detained, arrested, and imprisoned for charges most of the world recognizes as illegitimate. The tweets categorized as war crimes and crimes against humanity focus on situations and events that are not typically covered in the Western press: the 2015 military operations in southeastern Turkey against suspected PKK militants and Turkish involvement in the fighting in northern Syria.

Events

Events included tweets about specific happenings, including (1) domestic security–related events, such as police raids of HDP offices or military shelling of Kurdish towns in the southeast of Turkey; (2) events in Syria; (3) legal events, such as the arrests, detainments, and imprisonments of HDP leaders; (4) hunger strikes; (5) the attempted coup; and (6) COVID-19. The focus on events is especially important, as they are often discussing events that will not be part of the mainstream Turkish news narrative. They bring to light the shelling of civilians in Kurdish regions of Turkey and violent police actions taken against the party and its supporters. They include descriptions of events taking place in Syria that are presented with a very different perspective than that of the Turkish government. They tell of the arrests, detainments, imprisonments of the HDP leadership, MPs, mayors, and other activists on drummed-up charges of supporting terrorism, violence, separatism, and the PKK. HDP tweets inform followers of the hunger strikes of HDP leaders such as Layla Güven and the international attention it garnered. Twitter was one of the platforms used to communicate the HDPs strong opposition to 2016's attempted coup against the Turkish government. More recently, it has even been used to report on the pandemic and its effects on the Turkish population.

Rhetoric

Rhetoric was constructed from the language of the tweets. It includes language focusing on (1) fights and struggles, (2) calls to action, (3) messages of solidarity, (4) grieving and the loss of life, (5) hope, and (6) condemnation. The rhetoric that included calls to action; continuation of political, cultural, moral, and legal struggles; group solidarity; hope; and the condemnation of oppression is consistent with how the HDP defines itself. These themes within their messaging communicate the values of the organization.

People/actors

The fourth broad category is people/actors, which includes tweets about specific people, such as HDP leader Selahattin Demirtaş, Turkish president Recep Tayyip Erdoğan, or PKK leader Abdullah Öcalan. It also included other political parties, such as the AKP. The people/actors category was complicated by the massive presence of Demirtaş. Over one-third of all the cases in the study included the name Demirtaş in the tweet. The 1,042 tweets that included Demirtaş dwarfed those of any other actor. His one-time cochair and fellow political prisoner Figen Yüksekdağ is mentioned in 368 tweets, and Erdoğan is third at 91. This does, however, make a very powerful statement about the importance of Demirtaş to the party and the movement. Even though he is imprisoned and no longer serving as chair of the party, his presence and its symbolism are pervasive. The most retweeted tweet in the study was a quote from Demirtaş the day after he was arrested, "Fear may be contagious; but so is courage," retweeted 759 times by different users.

As the pro-Kurdish party, one might think that HDP tweets would often feature words like Kurd, Kurdish, Kurdistan, or even Kurdish cultural holidays, such as Newroz (Kurdish New Year) or Kurdish symbols of resistance like Kawa the blacksmith, but that sort of Kurdish identification is much more subtle. Only 203 tweets include those keywords, less than 7% of all cases. However, to anyone with knowledge of the HDP and Turkey, Kurdish issues are everywhere. The majority of tweets deal with issues, events, and actors that are related to Kurdish interests, when we take into account how these interests include human rights, democracy, peace, and justice.

Testimony as resistance

It should be noted that many of the tweets categorized under both human rights and events include horrific examples of violence against civilians and many accounts of the killing of children. These graphic, but not gratuitous, descriptions are disturbing to read, but add to the urgency of the HDP messaging. As noted in the literature review, narratives of victimization are an important strategy for human rights activists. Surprisingly, the formatting restrictions of Twitter as a platform do not prevent these powerful narratives from being communicated. In some ways, the brevity required grabs the reader's attention (and emotions) more effectively than a traditional, long-form narrative might.

4.11 Study limitations and conclusion

While this study does not look at HDP messaging in Turkish, we consulted with a native speaker fluent in both Turkish and English. After comparing our data set with the Turkish HDP Twitter account, it was confirmed that the content of the messaging in English was "about the same" as the messaging in Turkish.[95] This study focused entirely on the language of HDP messaging and did not delve into the content of websites, videos, or images posted within the tweets analyzed. Further analysis of these types of media may enhance or mediate our conclusions about what issues are considered most salient to audiences. Twitter reports that X number of tweets are removed from their platform based on government requests. In Turkey, this amounts to X tweets per year, although we have no way of knowing how many, if any, of HDPs tweets were removed during the time frame covered in our study. It would seem likely that HDPs messaging would be self-censored before publication to avoid removal and other, far more dangerous, consequences for violating Turkey's restriction on political speech, perhaps more so on their Turkish-language Twitter feed than their English page.

We can see through this content analysis that Twitter is used by the HDP not just to mobilize supporters, but to create community, express values, and educate followers. The HDP's use of social media fits neatly into what Watts refers to as a "loudspeaker system"[96] that allows pro-Kurdish voices to transmit highly contentions information politics that challenge the narratives promoted by the Turkish state institutions and creates a more "durable movement infrastructure." With Kurdish voices being shut out of the political discourse in Turkey, social media remains one of the few platforms the HDP has left. The Kurdish issue in Turkey is not going to fade away, especially as "Kurdish rights" and autonomy are being expressed and experienced in both Iraq and Syria. Pushing the HDP out of Turkish politics will simply lead to either another party rising up to fill the void, or the fight for identity and cultural rights will be left to more radical voices. As the fight for control and censorship of social media becomes part of the battle, it is important to pay attention to both the ways political actors communicate and what messages are being communicated.

The current moves to silence Twitter in Turkey are not new. The Turkish government has a habit of periodically blocking social media sites, typically after events that may paint the government in a negative light. The government has also used Twitter users' tweets against them. In 2016, following the failed coup attempt, no less than 55 people were imprisoned based on their Twitter and Facebook posts. Turkey also blocks access to social media sites through what is called "throttling," which slows down websites to the point of making them unusable.[97] Erdoğan has called Twitter a scourge he has promised to eradicate and called social media, in general, a menace to society.[98] Perhaps this is why Turkey accounts for 31% of all legal demands for removal requests to remove content on Twitter.[99]

The HDP is in a precarious position as of the writing of this piece. They are the third most popular party in Turkey, yet the AKP government's assault on the party and the party's leadership has put them in a difficult position. The current leader of the AKP allied Nationalist Movement Party (MHP), which is the fourth biggest party in Turkey, is calling for the banning of the HDP, accusing them of supporting separatism.[100] While many have expected the party to be banned, as has so often happened with Kurdish-dominated parties in the past, the Erdoğan regime seems set on destroying it with mass arrests and attempting to falsely tie the party's leaders to terrorism. The weaponizing of Turkey's judicial system, leading to most of the HDP's leadership, HDP elected officials, and 16,000 HDP members being arrested or detained, seems to indicate that the AKP strategy might work.[101]

Kurdish nationalism was born at the end of the 19th century; the Kurdish national movement in Turkey has been defined by the conflict between the Turkish state and the PKK since the 1980s, but today, legal political parties, although under attack, offer a path to cultural rights and greater autonomy without violence. The HDP has carved out a location in the Turkish polity to express progressive, socially democratic, human rights–oriented cultural identities, including Kurdish. By focusing so much of their communication on human rights and human rights–related issues, they are able to represent both Kurdish cultural rights and the interests of all Turkish citizens who want a more peaceful, democratic, and just Turkey.

Notes

1 M. Gunter, *The Kurds: A modern history* (Princeton: Markus Wiener, 2016); M. J. Totten, "The trouble with Turkey: Erdogan ISIS and the Kurds," *World Affairs* 178, no. 3 (2015); J. C. Randal, *Kurdistan: After such knowledge what forgiveness?* (London: Bloomsbury, 1998).
2 Donald McDowall, *A modern history of the Kurds* (London, England: I B Tauris, 2004).
3 G. Chaliand and M. Pallis, *A people without a country: The Kurds and Kurdistan* (New York: Olive Branch Press, 1993), 5.
4 D. Natali, *The Kurds and the state: Evolving national identity in Iraq, Turkey, and Iran* (Syracuse, NY: Syracuse University Press, 2005).
5 M. Weiss, "From constructive engagement to renewed estrangement? Securitization and Turkey's deteriorating relations with its Kurdish minority," *Turkish Studies* 17, no. 4 (2016): 571, https://doi.org/10.1080/14683849.016. 1228456.
6 Natali, *The Kurds and the State: Evolving National Identity in Iraq, Turkey, and Iran*; A. Marcus, *Blood and belief: The PKK and the Kurdish fight for independence* (Chesham: Combined Academic, 2007); Weiss, "From constructive engagement to renewed estrangement? Securitization and Turkey's deteriorating relations with its Kurdish minority"; N. Christofis, "The state of the Kurds in Erdoğan's 'new' Turkey," *Journal of Balkan & Near Eastern Studies* 21, no. 3 (2019): 251–259, https://doi.org/10.1080/19448953.2018.1497750; Totten, "The trouble with Turkey: Erdogan ISIS and the Kurds."
7 Totten, "The trouble with Turkey: Erdogan ISIS and the Kurds"; Cengiz Güneş, *Kurdish national movement in Turkey: From protest to resistance* (London: Routledge, 2012).
8 Christofis, "The state of the Kurds in Erdoğan's 'new' Turkey."
9 M. M. Gunter, "Erdogan's backsliding: Opposition to the KRG referendum," *Middle East Policy* 25, no. 1 (2018): 96–103.
10 Marcus, *Blood and belief: The PKK and the Kurdish fight for independence*; Ö. Celep, "The moderation of Turkey's Kurdish Left: The Peoples' Democratic Party HDP," *Turkish Studies* 19, no. 5 (2018): 723–747.
11 N. F. Watts, *Activists in office: Kurdish politics and protest in Turkey* (Seattle, WA: University of Washington Press, 2011); Güneş, *Kurdish national movement in Turkey: From protest to resistance*.
12 Marcus, *Blood and belief: The PKK and the Kurdish fight for independence*.
13 Marcus, *Blood and belief: The PKK and the Kurdish fight for independence*, 9.
14 J. Jongerden and A Akkaya, "Born from the left: The making of the PKK," in M. Casier and J. Jongerden (eds.), *Nationalisms and politics in Turkey: Political Islam, Kemalism and the Kurdish issue* (Milton Park Abingdon Oxon: Routledge, 2014).
15 Watts, *Activists in office: Kurdish politics and protest in Turkey*; E. J. Zürcher, *Turkey: A modern history* (London: I.B. Tauris, 2004).

16 Kendal Nezan, *The Kurds current position and historical background*, ed. Philip Kreyenbroek and Christine Allison (Atlantic Highlands, NJ: Zed Books, 1996), 15.
17 Marcus, *Blood and belief: The PKK and the Kurdish fight for independence*.
18 "Berxwedan: Documents from the Kurdish National Liberation Struggle," 1997, http://burn.ucsd.edu/ats/berxwedan.html.
19 M Gunter, "Reopening Turkey's closed Kurdish opening?" *Middle East Policy* 20, no. 2 (2013): 88–98, https://doi.org/10.1111/mepo.
20 Celep, "The moderation of Turkey's Kurdish Left: The Peoples' Democratic Party HDP"; Gunter, "Reopening Turkey's closed Kurdish opening?"
21 M. Glasman, "No friends but the mountains, " *The New Statesman* 148, no. 5493 (2019).
22 Marcus, *Blood and belief: The PKK and the Kurdish fight for independence*.
23 Gunter, *The Kurds: A modern history*, 123.
24 K. F. Toktamis, "A peace that wasn't: Friends, foes, and contentious re-entrenchment of Kurdish politics in Turkey," *Turkish Studies* 19, no. 5 (2018), https://doi.org/10.1080/14683849.2018.1500139.
25 Gunter, *The Kurds: A modern history*; Toktamis, "A peace that wasn't: Friends, foes, and contentious re-entrenchment of Kurdish politics in Turkey."
26 Ö. Celep, "Can the Kurdish Left contribute to Turkey's democratization?" *Insight Turkey* 16, no. 3 (2014): 165–180.
27 Celep, "The moderation of Turkey's Kurdish Left: The Peoples' Democratic Party HDP."
28 Watts, *Activists in office: Kurdish politics and protest in Turkey*.
29 The Guardian, "Turkey election 2015: Kurdish Obama is the country's bright new star," *The Guardian* (2015), https://www.theguardian.com/world/2015/jun/08/turkey-election-2015-kurdish-obama-is-the-countrys-bright-new-star.
30 Gunter, "Erdogan's backsliding: Opposition to the KRG referendum."
31 W. Gourlay, "The Kurds and the 'others': Kurdish politics as an inclusive multi-ethnic vehicle in Turkey," *Turkey Journal of Muslim Minority Affairs* 38, no. 4 (2018): 475–492, https://doi.org/10.1080/13602004.2018.1541300; Weiss, "From constructive engagement to renewed estrangement? Securitization and Turkey's deteriorating relations with its Kurdish minority"; Celep, "The moderation of Turkey's Kurdish Left: The Peoples' Democratic Party HDP"; *Guardian*, "Turkey election 2015: Kurdish Obama is the country's bright new star"; "HDP 2015 election manifesto: The great humanity we're all to the assembly," *Turkish Studies* 19, no. 5 (n.d.): 723–747, https://doi.org/10.1080/14683849.2018.1483195.
32 Weiss, "From constructive engagement to renewed estrangement? Securitization and Turkey's deteriorating relations with its Kurdish minority."
33 Gourlay, "The Kurds and the 'others': Kurdish politics as an inclusive multi-ethnic vehicle in Turkey."
34 *Guardian*, "Turkey election 2015: Kurdish Obama is the country's bright new star."
35 Weiss, "From constructive engagement to renewed estrangement? Securitization and Turkey's deteriorating relations with its Kurdish minority."
36 Gourlay, "The Kurds and the 'others': Kurdish politics as an inclusive multi-ethnic vehicle in Turkey."
37 Gunter, *The Kurds: A modern history*.
38 K. A. Cavanaugh, "Turkey's hidden wars," *Harvard Human Rights Journal* 31 (2018): 33–62.

39 K. Shaheen, *November 4 Turkey Arrests Pro-Kurdish Party Leaders Amid Claims of Internet Shutdown* (2016), https://www.theguardian.
40 Gunter, *The Kurds: A modern history*.
41 Human Rights Watch. (1997). Turkey. https://www.hrw.org/reports/1997/WR97/HELSINKI-17.htm#P674ð209013
42 *Hurriyet Daily News*, "Erdoğan: Gülenists PKK 'Armenian brigands' YPG tarred with the same brush," *Turkey News* (June 17, 2016), https://www.hurriyetdailynews.com/erdogan-gulenists-pkk-armenian-brigands-ypg-tarred-with-the-same-brush-100617.
43 V. Baird, "Betrayed again," *New Internationalist* 526 (2020): 15–20.
44 Human Rights Watch, "Turkey: Kurdish mayors' removal violates voters rights," *Human Rights Watch* (2020), https://www.hrw.org/news/2020/02/07/turkey-kurdish-mayors-removal-violates-voters-rights.
45 A. Kucukgocmen, "European court of human rights says Turkey must free Demirtas," (2020), https://www.reuters.com/article/us-turkey-echr-demirtas/european-court-of-human-rights-says-turkey-must-free-demirtas-idUSKBN28W1PJ.
46 Celep, "The moderation of Turkey's Kurdish Left: The Peoples' Democratic Party HDP."
47 Weiss, "From constructive engagement to renewed estrangement? Securitization and Turkey's deteriorating relations with its Kurdish minority."
48 Gunter, *The Kurds: A modern history*.
49 Gunter, "Erdogan's backsliding: Opposition to the KRG referendum."
50 Totten, "The trouble with Turkey: Erdogan ISIS and the Kurds."
51 Weiss, "From constructive engagement to renewed estrangement? Securitization and Turkey's deteriorating relations with its Kurdish minority."
52 Totten, "The trouble with Turkey: Erdogan ISIS and the Kurds."
53 The United Nations, "Universal declaration of human rights."
54 Ministry of Foreign Affairs, "Universal declaration of human rights," *Republic of Turkey*, accessed February 1, 2021, http://www.mfa.gov.tr/universal-declaration-of-human-rights.en.mfa.
55 Ranjoo Seodu Herr, "Women's rights as human rights and cultural imperialism," *Feminist Formations* 31, no. 3 (2019): 118–142, https://doi.org/10.1353/ff.2019.0033.
56 Kathryn Sikkink, "Human rights: Advancing the frontier of emancipation," *Development* 61, no. 1 (December 1, 2018): 14–20, https://doi.org/10.1057/s41301-018-0186-1.
57 Charles R. Beitz, *The idea of human rights*, 1st ed. (Oxford: Oxford University Press, 2011).
58 Elif M. Babül, "Radical once more: The contentious politics of human rights in Turkey," *Social Anthropology* 28, no. 1 (2020): 50–65, https://doi.org/10.1111/1469-8676.12740.
59 Weiss, "From constructive engagement to renewed estrangement? Securitization and Turkey's deteriorating relations with its Kurdish minority."
60 Babül, "Radical once more."
61 Başak Can, "Human rights, humanitarianism, and state violence: Medical documentation of torture in Turkey," *Medical Anthropology Quarterly* 30, no. 3 (September 2016): 342–358, https://doi.org/10.1111/maq.12259; Babül, "Radical Once More."

62. Ari Gandsman, "Narrative, human rights and the ethnographic reproduction of conventional knowledge," *Anthropologica* 55, no. 1 (2013): 130.
63. B. McKernan, "Turkey: The rise and fall of the Kurdish party that threatened Erdoğan" (2020), https://www.theguardian.com/world/2020/dec/27/as-erdogan-tightens-grip-on-power-last-opposition-politicians-resist-brutal-purge.
64. Statista, "Turkey: Social network penetration 2019," 2021, https://www.statista.com/statistics/284503/turkey-social-network-penetration/.
65. C. Sezer and D. Butler, "Turkey slaps ad ban on Twitter under new social media law," *Reuters*, https://www.reuters.com/article/us-turkey-twitter/turkey-slaps-ad-ban-on-twitter-under-new-social-media-law-idUSKBN29O0CT2021.
66. Sebastian Stier, Arnim Bleier, Haiko Lietz, Markus, Strohmaier. "Election campaigning on social media: Politicians, audiences, and the mediation of political communication," *Political Communication* 35 (2008): 50–74, https://doi.org/10.1080/10584609.2017.1334728; Anders Olof Larsson and Eli Skogerbø, "Out with the old, in with the new? Perceptions of social (and other) media by local and regional Norwegian politicians," *New Media & Society* 20, no. 1 (January 1, 2018): 219–236, https://doi.org/10.1177/1461444816661549.
67. Daniela V. Dimitrova and Jörg Matthes, "Social media in political campaigning around the world: Theoretical and methodological challenges," *Journalism & Mass Communication Quarterly* 95, no. 2 (June 1, 2018): 333–342, https://doi.org/10.1177/1077699018770437; Andreas Jungherr, "Twitter use in election campaigns: A systematic literature review," *Journal of Information Technology & Politics* 13, no. 1 (January 2, 2016): 72–91, https://doi.org/10.1080/19331681.2015.1132401; Y. T. Alfarhoud, "The use of Twitter as a tool to predict opinion leaders that influence public opinion: Case study of the 2016 United State presidential election," in J Allen, D Alemneh, and S Hawamdeh (eds.), *Knowledge discovery and data design innovation*, vol. 14, Series on Innovation and Knowledge Management (Dallas, TX: World Scientific, 2017), 191–206, https://doi.org/10.1142/9789813234482_0010.
68. Jungherr, "Twitter use in election campaigns."
69. Galen Stolee and Steve Caton, "Twitter, Trump, and the base: A shift to a new form of presidential talk?" *Signs and Society* 6, no. 1 (January 1, 2018): 147–165, https://doi.org/10.1086/694755.
70. Dimitrova and Matthes, "Social media in political campaigning around the world."
71. Maxwell E. McCombs and Donald L. Shaw, "The agenda-setting function of mass media," *The Public Opinion Quarterly* 36, no. 2 (1972): 176–187.
72. P. F. Lazarsfeld, B. Berelson, and H. Gaudet, *The people's choice* (Oxford, England: Duell, Sloan & Pearce, 1944).
73. McCombs and Shaw, "The agenda-setting function of mass media."
74. Bernard Cohen, *Press and foreign policy* (Princeton: Princeton University Press, 1963), https://www.jstor.org/stable/j.ctt183q0fp.
75. Maxwell E. McCombs, Donald L. Shaw and David H. Weaver, "New directions in agenda-setting theory and research," *Mass Communication and Society* 17, no. 6 (November 2, 2014): 781–802, https://doi.org/10.1080/15205436.2014.964871.
76. John Parmelee, "The agenda-building function of political tweets," *New Media & Society* 16 (April 2, 2013): 434–450, https://doi.org/10.1177/1461444813487955.
77. Alfarhoud, "The use of Twitter as a tool to predict opinion leaders that influence public opinion."

78 Parmelee, "The agenda-building function of political tweets."
79 Herbert Gans, *Deciding what's news: A study of CBS evening news, NBC nightly news, Newsweek, and time* (Evanston, IL: Northwestern University Press, 1980), https://scholar.google.com/scholar_lookup?hl=en&publication_year=19 80&author=Herbert+Gans&title=+Deciding+What+is+News+.
80 Karen M. Lancendorfer and Byoungkwan Lee, "Who influences whom? The agenda-building relationship between political candidates and the media in the 2002 Michigan governor's race," *Journal of Political Marketing* 9, no. 3 (July 30, 2010): 186–206, https://doi.org/10.1080/15377857.2010.497737.
81 Parmelee, "The agenda-building function of political tweets."
82 Chinenye Nwabueze and Ebere Okonkwo, "Rethinking the bullet theory in the digital age," *International Journal of Media, Journalism and Mass Communications* 4, no. 2 (2018): 1–10, https://doi.org/10.20431/2454-9479.0402001.
83 Berelson Lazarsfeld and Gaudet, *The people's choice*; Elihu Katz, "The two-step flow of communication: An up-to-date report on an hypothesis," *Public Opinion Quarterly* 21, no. 1, Anniversary Issue Devoted to Twenty Years of Public Opinion Research (1957): 61, https://doi.org/10.1086/266687.
84 Marton Bene, "Post shared, vote shared: investigating the link between Facebook performance and electoral success during the Hungarian general election campaign of 2014," *Journalism & Mass Communication Quarterly* 95, no. 2 (June 1, 2018): 363–380, https://doi.org/10.1177/1077699018763309.
85 Sujin Choi, "The two-step flow of communication in Twitter-based public forums," *Social Science Computer Review* 33, no. 6 (December 1, 2015): 696–711, https://doi.org/10.1177/0894439314556599.
86 Alfarhoud, "The use of Twitter as a tool to predict opinion leaders that influence public opinion."
87 Stier et al., "Election campaigning on social media: Politicians, audiences, and the mediation of political communication."
88 Stier et al., "Election campaigning on social media: Politicians, audiences, and the mediation of political communication," 73.
89 Alexander Halavis, "Bigger sociological imaginations: Framing big social data theory and methods," *Information, Communication & Society* 18, no 5 (2015): 583–594; Jungherr, "Twitter use in election campaigns"; C. Schnider, "The biggest data challenges that you might not even know you have," *IBM, Watson* (May 25, 2016), https://www.ibm.com/blogs/watson/2016/05/biggest-data-challenges-might-not-even-know/.
90 Derrick Cogburn, "Big data analytics and text mining in internet governance research: Computational analysis of transcripts from 12 years of the internet governance forum," in Laura DeNardis, Nanette S. Levinson and Francesca Musiani (eds.), *Researching internet governance: Methods, frameworks, futures* (The MIT Press, 2020), https://doi.org/10.7551/mitpress/12400.003.0010.
91 Nadra Pencle and Irina Mălăescu, "What's in the words? Development and validation of a multidimensional dictionary for CSR and application using prospectuses," *Journal of Emerging Technologies in Accounting* 13, no. 2 (2016): 109–127; C. Hughes, "Thou art in a deal: The evolution of religious language in the public communications of Donald Trump," *International Journal of Communication* 14, no. 2 (2020); M. Laver and J. Garry, "Estimating policy positions from political texts," *American Journal of Political Science* 44, no. 3 (2000): 619–634.

92 D. Marina et al., "Industry-specific CSR: Analysis of 20 years of research," *European Business Review* 28, no. 3 (2016): 250–273.
93 The United Nations, "Universal declaration of human rights."
94 The United Nations, "OHCHR | International covenant on economic, social and cultural rights," 1966, https://www.ohchr.org/EN/ProfessionalInterest/Pages/CESCR.aspx; The United Nations, "OHCHR | International covenant on civil and political rights," 1966, https://www.ohchr.org/en/professionalinterest/pages/ccpr.aspx; The United Nations, "Framework of analysis for atrocity crimes: A tool for prevention," 2014, https://www.globalr2p.org/resources/framework-of-analysis-for-atrocity-crimes-a-tool-for-prevention/; Beitz, *The idea of human rights*; Babül, "Radical once more."
95 Thanks go to Mustafa Karadeniz for his comparative analysis of the two Twitter pages.
96 Watts, *Activists in office: Kurdish politics and protest in Turkey*.
97 Reuters, "Turkey blocks access to Twitter WhatsApp: Internet monitoring group" (2016), https://www.reuters.com/article/us-turkey-security-internet-idUSKBN12Z0H4/.
98 D. Bernard, *Turkey moves to block internet access voice of America* (Voice of America, 2017), https://www.voanews.com/europe/turkey-moves-block-internet-access.
99 Twitter Transparency Center, "Turkey report," *Twitter Transparency Center*, 2020, https://transparency.twitter.com/en/reports/countries/tr.html.
100 D. Butler, "Erdogan ally calls for Turkey's pro-Kurdish party to be banned," *Reuters* (2020), https://www.reuters.com/article/turkey-politics-kurds-int/erdogan-ally-calls-for-turkeys-pro-kurdish-party-to-be-banned-idUSKBN-28R1EJ.
101 McKernan, *Turkey: The rise and fall of the Kurdish party that threatened Erdoğan*.

References

Agence France-Presse. (2015, June 7). Turkey election 2015: Kurdish Obama is the country's bright new star. *The Guardian*. https://www.theguardian.com/world/2015/jun/08/turkey-election-2015-kurdish-obama-is-the-countrys-bright-new-star

Alfarhoud, Y. T. (2017). The use of Twitter as a tool to predict opinion leaders that influence public opinion: Case study of the 2016 United State presidential election. In J. Allen, D. Alemneh, & S. Hawamdeh (Eds.), *Knowledge discovery and data design innovation* (Vol. 14, pp. 191–206). World Scientific.

Baird, V. (2020, June 22). The Kurds: Betrayed again. *New Internationalist, 526*, 15–20. https://newint.org/features/2020/06/11/big-story-kurds-betrayed-again

Beitz, C. R. (2011). *The idea of human rights* (1st ed.). Oxford University Press.

Bene, M. (2018). Post shared, vote shared: Investigating the link between Facebook performance and electoral success during the Hungarian general election campaign of 2014. *Journalism & Mass Communication Quarterly, 95*(2), 363–380.

Bernard, D. (2017, January 4). *Turkey moves to block internet access.* Voice of America. https://www.voanews.com/europe/turkey-moves-block-internet-access
Berxwedan: Documents from the Kurdish National Liberation Struggle. (n.d.). Retrieved April, 25, 1997, from http://burn.ucsd.edu/~ats/berxwedan.html
Butler, D. (2020, December 17). Erdogan ally calls for Turkey's pro-Kurdish party to be banned. *Reuters.* https://www.reuters.com/article/turkey-politics-kurds-int/erdogan-ally-calls-for-turkeys-pro-kurdish-party-to-be-banned-idUSKBN-28R1EJ
Can, B. (2016). Human rights, humanitarianism, and state violence: Medical documentation of torture in Turkey. *Medical Anthropology Quarterly, 30*(3), 342–358.
Cavanaugh, K. A. (2018). Turkey's hidden wars. *Harvard Human Rights Journal, 31,* 33–62.
Celep, Ö. (2014). Can the Kurdish Left contribute to Turkey's democratization? *Insight Turkey, 16*(3), 165–180.
Celep, Ö. (2018). The moderation of Turkey's Kurdish Left: The peoples' democratic party HDP. *Turkish Studies, 19*(5), 723–747.
Cengiz, G. (2012). *Kurdish national movement in Turkey: From protest to resistance.* Routledge.
Chaliand, G., & Pallis, M. (1993). *A people without a country: The Kurds and Kurdistan.* Olive Branch Press.
Choi, S. (2015). The two-step flow of communication in Twitter-based public forums. *Social Science Computer Review, 33*(6), 696–711.
Christofis, N. (2019). The state of the Kurds in Erdoğan's 'new' Turkey. *Journal of Balkan & Near Eastern Studies, 21*(3), 251–259.
Çiçek, C. (2018). The failed resolution process and the transformation of Kurdish. *Politics Middle East Report, 48*(3), 19–24.
Cogburn, D. (2020). Big data analytics and text mining in internet governance research: Computational analysis of transcripts from 12 years of the internet governance forum. In L. DeNardis, N. S. Levinson, & F. Musiani (Eds.), *Researching internet governance: Methods, frameworks, futures.* The MIT Press.
Cohen, B. (1963). *Press and foreign policy.* Princeton University Press.
Dimitrova, D. V., & Matthes, J. (2018). Social media in political campaigning around the world: Theoretical and methodological challenges. *Journalism & Mass Communication Quarterly, 95*(2), 333–342.
Glasman, M. (2019, October 16). *No friends but the mountains.* New Statesman. https://www.newstatesman.com/world/middle-east/2019/10/no-friends-mountains
Gourlay, W. (2018). The Kurds and the "others": Kurdish politics as an inclusive multi-ethnic vehicle. *Turkey Journal of Muslim Minority Affairs, 38*(4), 475–492.
Güneş, C. (2012). *The Kurdish national movement in Turkey: From protest to resistance.* Routledge.
Gunter, M. (2013). Reopening Turkey's closed Kurdish opening? *Middle East Policy, 20*(2), 88–98.
Gunter, M. (2016). *The Kurds: A modern history.* Markus Wiener Publishers.
Gunter, M. (2018). Erdogan's backsliding: Opposition to the KRG referendum. *Middle East Policy, 25*(1), 96–103.

Halavis, A. (2015). Bigger sociological imaginations: Framing big social data theory and methods. *Information, Communication & Society*, *18*(5), 583–594.

Herr, R. S. (2019). Women's rights as human rights and cultural imperialism. *Feminist Formations*, *31*(3), 118–142.

Hughes, C. (2020). Thou art in a deal: The evolution of religious language in the public communications of Donald Trump. *International Journal of Communication*, *14*(2).

Human Rights Watch. (1994). *Turkey*. https://www.hrw.org/reports/1994/WR94/Helsinki-21.htm#P680ō209831

Human Rights Watch. (2020, February 7). *Turkey: Kurdish mayors' removal violates voters' rights*. https://www.hrw.org/news/2020/02/07/turkey-kurdish-mayors-removal-violates-voters-rights

Human Rights Watch. (2020). *Turkey*. https://www.hrw.org/reports/1997/WR97/HELSINKI-17.htm#P674ō209013

Hurriyet Daily News. (2016, June 17). *Erdoğan: Gülenists PKK 'Armenian brigands' YPG tarred with the same brush*. https://www.hurriyetdailynews.com/erdogan-gulenists-pkk-armenian-brigands-ypg-tarred-with-the-same-brush-100617

Jongerden, J., & Akkaya, A. (2014). Born from the left: The making of the PKK. In M. Casier & J. Jongerden (Eds.), *Nationalisms and politics in Turkey: Political Islam, Kemalism and the Kurdish issue*. Routledge.

Jungherr, A. (2016). Twitter use in election campaigns: A systematic literature review. *Journal of Information Technology & Politics*, *13*(1), 72–91.

Katz, E. (1957). The two-step flow of communication: An up-to-date report on a hypothesis. *Public Opinion Quarterly*, *21*(1, Anniversary Issue Devoted to Twenty Years of Public Opinion Research), 61.

Kucukgocmen, A. (2020, December 22). European court of human rights says Turkey must free Demirtas. *Reuters*. https://www.reuters.com/article/us-turkey-echr-demirtas/european-court-of-human-rights-says-turkey-must-free-demirtas-idUSKBN28W1PJ

Lancendorfer, K. M., & Lee, B. (2010). Who influences whom? The agenda-building relationship between political candidates and the media in the 2002 Michigan governor's race. *Journal of Political Marketing*, *9*(3), 186–206.

Larsson, A. O., & Skogerbø, E. (2018). Out with the old, in with the new? Perceptions of social (and other) media by local and regional Norwegian politicians. *New Media & Society*, *20*(1), 219–236.

Laver, M., & Garry, J. (2000). Estimating policy positions from political texts. *American Journal of Political Science*, *44*(3), 619–634.

Lazarsfeld, P. F., Berelson, B., & Gaudet, H. (1949). *The people's choice*. Columbia University Press.

Marcus, A. (2007). *Blood and belief: The PKK and the Kurdish fight for independence*. New York University Press.

Marina, D., Ana, C., Olivier, L., Mollie, P.-M., & Silvana, B. (2016). Industry-specific CSR: analysis of 20 years of research. *European Business Review*, *28*(3), 250–273.

McCombs, M. E., & Shaw, D. L. (1972). The agenda-setting function of mass media. *The Public Opinion Quarterly, 36*(2), 176–187.
McCombs, M. E., Shaw, D. L., & Weaver, D. H. (2014). New directions in agenda-setting theory and research. *Mass Communication and Society, 17*(6), 781–802.
McDowall, D. (2004). *A modern history of the Kurds*. I.B. Tauris.
McKernan, B. (2020, December 27). Turkey: The rise and fall of the Kurdish party that threatened Erdoğan. *The Guardian*. https://www.theguardian.com/world/2020/dec/27/as-erdogan-tightens-grip-on-power-last-opposition-politicians-resist-brutal-purge
Natali, D. (2005). *The Kurds and the state: Evolving national identity in Iraq, Turkey, and Iran*. Syracuse University Press.
New Internationalist. (2020, July 31). *100 years of hope, struggle and betrayal*. https://newint.org/features/2020/06/11/100-years-hope-struggle-and-betrayal
Nezan, K. (1996). The Kurds current position and historical background. In P. Kreyenbroek & C. Allison (Eds.), *Kurdish Culture and Identity*. Zed Books.
Nwabueze, C., & Okonkwo, E. (2018). Rethinking the bullet theory in the digital age. *International Journal of Media, Journalism and Mass Communications, 4*(2), 1–10.
Parmelee, J. (2013). The agenda-building function of political tweets. *New Media & Society, 16*, 434–450.
Pencle, N., & Mălăescu, I. (2016). What's in the words? Development and validation of a multidimensional dictionary for CSR and application using prospectuses. *Journal of Emerging Technologies in Accounting, 13*(2), 109–127.
Randal, J. (1998). *Kurdistan: After such knowledge what forgiveness?* Bloomsbury.
Republic of Turkey Ministry of Foreign Affairs. (n.d.). *Universal declaration of human rights*. http://www.mfa.gov.tr/universal-declaration-of-human-rights.en.mfa
Reuters. (2016, November 4). *Turkey blocks access to Twitter Whatsapp: Internet monitoring group*. https://www.reuters.com/article/us-turkey-security-internet-idUSKBN12Z0H4/
Sezer, C., & Butler, D. (2021, January 19). Turkey slaps ad ban on Twitter under new social media law. *Reuters*. https://www.reuters.com/article/us-turkey-twitter/turkey-slaps-ad-ban-on-twitter-under-new-social-media-law-idUSKBN29O0CT
Shaheen, K. (2016, November 4). Turkey arrests pro-Kurdish party leaders amid claims of internet shutdown. *The Guardian*. https://www.theguardian.com/world/2016/nov/04/turkey-arrests-pro-kurdish-party-leaders-mps
Sikkink, K. (2018). Human rights: Advancing the frontier of emancipation. *Development, 61*(1), 14–20.
Statista. (2021). *Turkey: Social network penetration 2019*. https://www.statista.com/statistics/284503/turkey-social-network-penetration/
Stier, S., Bleier, A., Lietz, H., & Strohmaier, M. (2008). Election campaigning on social media: Politicians, audiences, and the mediation of political communication. *Political Communication, 35*, 50–74. https://doi.org/10.1080/10584609.2017.1334728

Toktamis, K. F. (2018). A peace that wasn't: Friends, foes, and contentious re-entrenchment of Kurdish politics in Turkey. *Turkish Studies, 19*(5).

Totten, M. J. (2015). The trouble with Turkey: Erdogan, ISIS, and the Kurds. *World Affairs, 178*(3).

Twitter Transparency Center. (2020). *Turkey report*. https://transparency.twitter.com/en/reports/countries/tr.html

The United Nations. (1948). *Universal declaration of human rights*. United Nations.

The United Nations. (1966a). *OHCHR | International covenant on civil and political rights*. https://www.ohchr.org/en/professionalinterest/pages/ccpr.aspx

The United Nations. (1966b). *OHCHR | International covenant on economic, social and cultural rights*. https://www.ohchr.org/EN/ProfessionalInterest/Pages/CESCR.aspx

The United Nations. (2014). *Framework of analysis for atrocity crimes: A tool for prevention*. https://www.globalr2p.org/resources/framework-of-analysis-for-atrocity-crimes-a-tool-for-prevention/

Watts, N. F. (2011). *Activists in office: Kurdish politics and protest in Turkey*. University of Washington Press.

Weiss, M. (2016). From constructive engagement to renewed estrangement? Securitization and Turkey's deteriorating relations with its Kurdish minority. *Turkish Studies, 17*(4), 567–598.

Zürcher, E. J. (2004). *Turkey: A modern history*. I.B. Tauris.

Appendix

Table 4A.1 Human rights topics frequency distribution

	Frequency	% Shown	% Processed	% Total	No. of cases	% Cases
Civil/political	2236	47.43%	7.74%	3.66%	1397	46.77%
War_crimes/crimes_against_humanity	1670	35.43%	5.78%	2.74%	1097	36.73%
Diversity/minority_rights	340	7.21%	1.18%	0.56%	231	7.73%
Human rights general	335	7.11%	1.16%	0.55%	285	9.54%
Economic/social/cultural	133	2.82%	0.46%	0.22%	115	3.85%

Table 4A.2 Human rights subtopics frequency distribution

	Frequency	% Shown	% Processed	% Total	No. of cases	% Cases
War_crimes	1544	32.54%	5.34%	2.53%	1024	34.28%
Judicial/legal	1030	21.71%	3.56%	1.69%	717	24.00%
Democracy/fair_elections	699	14.73%	2.42%	1.15%	543	18.18%
Human rights general	335	7.06%	1.16%	0.55%	285	9.54%
Women & children rights	309	6.51%	1.07%	0.51%	211	7.06%
Civil/pol_general	201	4.24%	0.70%	0.33%	177	5.93%
Authoritarianism	190	4.00%	0.66%	0.31%	165	5.52%
Crimes_against_humanity	153	3.22%	0.53%	0.25%	144	4.82%
Economic/social/cultural	133	2.80%	0.46%	0.22%	115	3.85%
Propaganda/free_speech	120	2.53%	0.42%	0.20%	89	2.98%
Racism	16	0.34%	0.06%	0.03%	12	0.40%
LGBTQ+_rights	15	0.32%	0.05%	0.02%	11	0.37%

Table 4.4.3 Human rights topics norm variations

	Frequency	% Shown	% Processed	% Total	No. of cases	% Cases	Expected	Deviation	Z	P(2-tails)
War_crimes/crimes_against_humanity	141	47.2%	9.4%	4.6%	71	48.0%	83.1	69.7%	6.38	0.000
Civil/political	132	44.2%	8.8%	4.4%	78	52.7%	111.3	18.6%	1.95	0.051
Human rights general	17	5.7%	1.1%	0.6%	13	8.8%	16.7	2.0%	-0.04	0.967
Diversity/minority_rights	5	1.7%	0.3%	0.2%	2	1.4%	16.9	-70.4%	-2.78	0.005
Economic/social/cultural	4	1.3%	0.3%	0.1%	4	2.7%	6.6	-39.6%	-0.82	0.410

Table 4A.4 Human rights subtopics norm variations

	Frequency	% Shown	% Processed	% Total cases		% Cases	Expected	Deviation	Z	P (2-tails)
War_crimes	135	45.00%	9.00%	4.50%	70	47.30%	83.1	69.70%	6.38	0
Judicial/legal	61	20.30%	4.10%	2.00%	46	31.10%	111.3	18.60%	1.95	0.051
Democracy/fair_elections	42	14.00%	2.80%	1.40%	28	18.90%	16.7	2.00%	-0.04	0.967
Human rights general	17	5.70%	1.10%	0.60%	13	8.80%	16.9	-70.40%	-2.78	0.005
Civil/pol_general	12	4.00%	0.80%	0.40%	11	7.40%	6.6	-39.60%	-0.82	0.410
Propaganda/free_speech	9	3.00%	0.60%	0.30%	6	4.10%	15.7	-49.10%	-1.83	0.068
Authoritarianism	8	2.70%	0.50%	0.30%	8	5.40%	3.4	45.60%	0.58	0.565
Crimes_against_humanity	7	2.30%	0.50%	0.20%	6	4.10%	4.2	-4.30%	0.16	0.875
Women & children rights	5	1.70%	0.30%	0.20%	2	1.40%				
Economic/social/cultural	4	1.30%	0.30%	0.10%	4	2.70%				

94 *Ned Rinalducci*

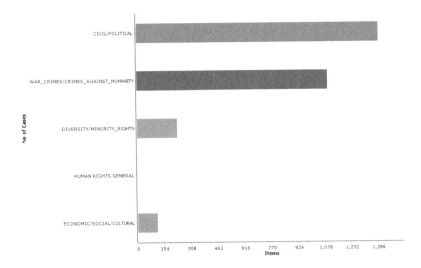

Figure 4A.1 Distribution of human topics

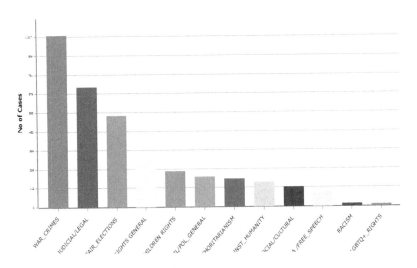

Figure 4A.2 Distribution of human rights subtopics

Kurdish resistance and agenda setting 95

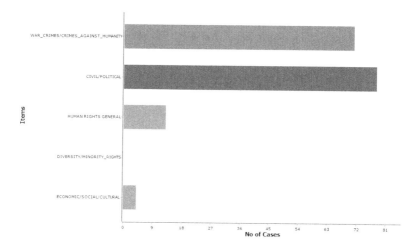

Figure 4A.3 Distribution of human rights topics for top 5% of retweets

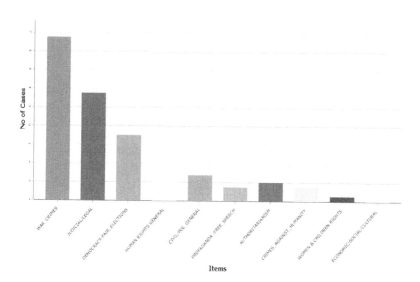

Figure 4A.4 Distribution of human rights subtopics for top 5% of retweets

5 Exploring the culture of digital resistance in India

The *Nirbhaya* effect

Nalanda Roy & Stephanie Mae-Pedron

5.1 Introduction

On December 16, 2012, a 23-year-old physiotherapy intern, Jyoti Singh, and her male friend, Awindra Pandey, were assaulted while riding a private bus in South Delhi, India. They were brutally beaten by six passengers riding the bus including the driver. While Pandey was left semiconscious, Singh was horrifically gang-raped and tortured with an iron rod. They were later thrown out onto the roadside after the attack, where they were eventually spotted by highway patrol and taken to the hospital.[1] The two received emergency medical treatment for their wounds. Pandey managed to survive, but the extent of Singh's injuries was far worse, and she succumbed to them 13 days later. Owing to laws against publishing the identity of a rape victim in India, Singh was bestowed the name, *Nirbhaya,* meaning "the fearless one."

The brutality of the wounds inflicted upon Singh and her highly publicized 13-day struggle for life that followed sparked widespread public outrage both on the ground and online. Modern communication technology made it possible for the rape to be covered by media outlets all around the globe. Mass coverage of the incident swiftly transformed it into something more than the cruel assault of a young woman. *Nirbhaya* became a humanitarian crisis, a symbol for women's rights movements to rally around. It was even considered to be India's "Arab Spring." Six people including the four convicts, Ram Singh, and a juvenile who were named as the main accused were arrested within a few days. The trial of the five adult men began in a special fast-track court in March 2013. Ram Singh, who was the prime accused, allegedly committed suicide by hanging himself in Tihar jail a few days after the trial began. The juvenile, who was said to be the most brutal of the attackers, was put in a correctional home for three years. After years of fight to get justice for *Nirbhaya,* in March 2020, the convicts were hanged to death.[2]

DOI: 10.4324/9781003109310-5

On the global stage,

the incident was taken up by One Billion Rising, a global campaign to end violence against women, where the number "billion" refers to the UN figure that approximately one billion, or one in every three women will be raped or beaten in their lifetime.[3]

On the domestic level, it was the final push that the Indian people needed to voice their objections regarding unreliable transportation, unsympathetic police, and mounting crime rates. Verbal dissent evolved into physical action as thousands of protestors took to the streets to participate in civil demonstrations and candlelight vigils to demand not only justice for *Nirbhaya*, but better conditions for all women in India. The internet played a vital role in both organizing and mobilizing the urban Delhi middle class.[4] Because communication technology has the capacity to both facilitate and hinder collaborative action, examining how these advanced modes of communication affected Indian society after the *Nirbhaya* incident is necessary in order to understand the impact of digital resistance on the public sphere, particularly their democratic potential for creating new opportunities for discourse that cannot be easily censored. This is especially important to consider in the context of India's conservative culture, which is still experiencing adjustment challenges to the educational and economic advances by women who have long been confined to the home.[5] In many societies, the endurance of rape myths is common. These false, but deeply ingrained notions have a direct effect on whether women report—or even speak about—an incidence of sexual assault.

This chapter analyzes the harnessing effect of digital media and how it affected public discourse and women's perceptions after the incident. To examine these subjects, drawing upon existing literature regarding violent crimes against women in India and in other countries, changes in Indian sexual assault laws, and statistical data covering reported rape cases and their conviction rates in India over the last decade can help paint a broader picture of the varying facets of such widespread publicity. This chapter also takes into consideration the impact of rape myths and skewed gender ratios on society as well as the former's possible implications on the legislative process.

5.2 The internet and modern communication technology

The internet is, arguably, the world's most populous sphere for public discourse. People's opinions now have the capacity to be known to a wide, largely anonymous audience. The worldwide web is convenient because it allows the masses to send and receive messages, participate in forums, share their viewpoints, and so on. While censorship may be an issue in certain countries or websites, functional workarounds that enable an individual to have their opinions digitally published continue to exist. The sheer abundance of messages, then, is an indication of democratic potential.[6] Furthermore, the internet, aided by modern methods of communication, has the unique ability to taper the distance between action and speech at an unparalleled rate by diversifying how information is spread and connecting likeminded people who can coordinate their activities on a broad scale. While it can be used for malicious purposes, the internet is considered to be a neutral space that is open to everyone with the equipment and technical knowledge to utilize it. In other words, cyberspace is a place for all people, including radical groups interested in expressing social and political discontent.[7] Although digital social ties are oftentimes merely online manifestations or expansions of offline, personal relationships, social networking services—like Facebook, Twitter, and Instagram—serve the dual purpose of charting (and strengthening) existing connections and constructing new ones. The internet can therefore be used to make both positive and negative contacts; the intent that people project onto virtual interactions is what makes the most difference when communicating.

The passive nature of the internet means that users often only discover what they seek.[8] According to a survey conducted in India, only an estimated 80% of individuals willfully received news from alternative sources that challenged their views. Figure 5.1 lists which alternative sources individuals would use to gain access to variant information.

Nevertheless, the unique ability for online information to go viral can make even initially uninterested individuals concerned about particular issues: vital social dilemmas or highly publicized criminal cases, for example. That users have instantaneous access to thousands of different news sources and related informational websites, as well as the capacity to converse with others in real time, also creates a harnessing effect among distant masses. In this way, the internet can help individuals become more active political participants.

In the case of India after the incident, dissent, especially among young people, became rampant. Over 80,000 people sent letters to their local governments with ideas regarding how to amend laws concerning sexual assault and suggestions related to improving security. Online activists began utilizing a black dot—amply dubbed the "black dot of shame"—to signify: (1) their relationship with the movement; (2) their anger at the perpetrators in the *Nirbhaya* case and the inhumane acts that they committed; (3) their collective shame from being a part of a society that wasn't doing enough

The culture of digital resistance 99

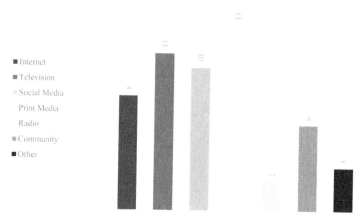

Figure 5.1 Alternative news sources

to protect women from such brutal acts; and (4) how they perceived the incident as a blemish on Indian society, as the "fault of an entire culture that was unsafe for women."[9] The black dot then, was a tacit expression of how *Nirbhaya* wasn't just an abrupt misfortune, but the culmination of countless long-standing issues that plagued their nation. Figure 5.2 breaks down data related to people's views on the varying implications of online symbols like the black dot of shame and hashtags.

People spread the black dot online via tweets—along with hashtags like #StopThisShame, #DelhiGangRape, #DelhiProtests—Facebook shares, and even by changing their account pictures on WhatsApp (a free, global instant messaging and video calling platform). Thus, information about the case rapidly disseminated. The symbol naturally sparked questions in people's minds, and asking about it afforded them the opportunity to learn more. Hashtags and other virtual marks serve to educate citizens and rouse support. They might even pave the way for interested citizens to join active, online forums discussing potential meetups. The visibility of the case was greatly enhanced through the simultaneous shares by users across several social media platforms. "It is estimated that the number of broadband connections in India is more than twice the size of the British general population . . . (with an estimated) 65 million Facebook users and 35 million Twitter accounts."[10] The symbol, along with news of the case, trended in a way that would be close to impossible without the highly interconnected digital networks available to people today. This extensive sharing ensured that even relatively low-information individuals or those only active on one

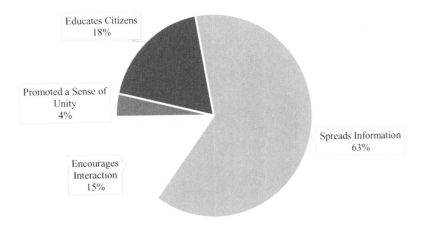

Figure 5.2 Significance of online symbols

network at least recognized the symbol. However, this form of swift digital media circulation is not without its drawbacks. There can be several explanations for why an individual decides to share information (or even valueless images/blocks of text), especially in a sphere as public as social media.

While some users understood the meaning behind the black dot and shared it in the hopes of getting others to participate in real-life civil protests, others might have only been doing it for the sense of unity it evoked within them. This abstract feeling of contribution through communicative action is described by political theorist Jodi Dean in her article, "Communicative Capitalism: Circulation and the Foreclosure of Politics," as a result of a registration effect, whereby people believed that they were actively stirring discussion or that they were making relevant contributions whenever they "clicked on a button, added their name to a petition, or commented on a blog."[11] For Dean, this suggested that certain activities on the internet involved a profound passivity and that communication technology may have distorted people's understanding of active involvement. There is also the possibility that users could have been mindlessly sharing the black dot because so many others were doing so in a common phenomenon known as the bandwagon effect. These users might not have even known most of the details surrounding the *Nirbhaya* incident and were simply sharing it for the sake of being able to say that they did. A basic design of communication is the message and the response to the message, but in cases such as this, messages end up becoming mere additions to broader discussions that don't necessarily require—or elicit—a response.[12] Their purpose becomes that of forwarding, and their original goal—that is, to spur discussion—deteriorates. In another article, Dean argues that the "astronomical increase in information generated by our searching, commenting, and participating entrap us in a setting of communication without communicability."[13] When this occurs, the value of messages shifts, and their meaning falls behind their ability to circulate. In other words, rather than prompting effective dialogue between two or more parties, the core action of the shared information becomes that of distribution.

The convenience of communication technology, then, also acts as a hindrance. While it may empower individuals with knowledge and the ability to communicate with distant people in real time, social movements and relatedly, social change, demand more than virtual connections. They demand sentiment and will. Emotions play a key role in an individual's involvement in political demonstrations, but without physical follow-up and without active, corporeal organization on the ground to supplement dissent online, protestors on the web can become ensnared in never-ending circles of non-participation. Figures 5.3, 5.4, and 5.5 are based on survey data that examined people's perceptions regarding the different (useful) functions, strengths, and hindrances of communication technology.

Additionally, individuals were asked to choose what they believed to be the most significant drawback to unlimited access to information. A majority believed that the general public consumed information at face value. This data is presented in Figure 5.6.

It is also important to consider how the simple act of sharing a message can spring a movement forward, as it more easily allows information to reach individuals who are interested in physically organizing or even simply writing letters to their local government. It has been established that digital networks and social media platforms can arouse feelings of unity between its users (Thompson, 2011). While this may not be enough to produce a physical community, these sentiments can become a catalyst for collective action.[14] Global social movements like #MeToo have shown how feelings of solidarity often arise among individuals who have gone through similar experiences. Owing to innovations in communication technology, these sentiments can now, more than ever before, quickly turn into a unified fight for social change. Online communication and sharing, despite the perfunctory forwarding done by certain users, may even become the primary form of reaching out to others as it did in India.

Whether these movements are sustainable, however, is highly dependent on the broader society, specifically, its political climate. Protest groups that find their thickest roots online typically form much quicker than their traditional counterparts. The results are often "flash protests" that break up just as suddenly as they form, especially when confronted with violence.

102 Nalanda Roy & Stephanie Mae-Pedron

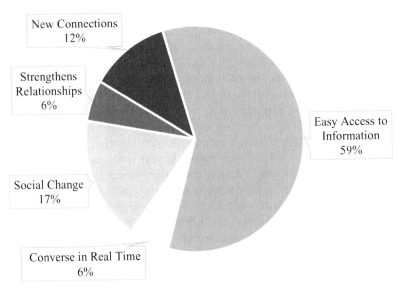

Figure 5.3 Most useful function of communication technology

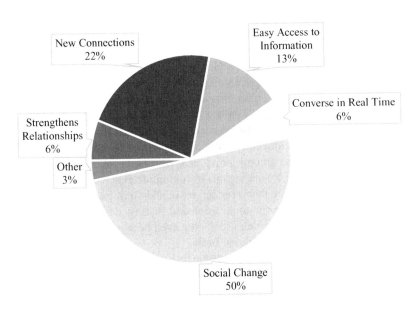

Figure 5.4 Strengthen relationships of communication technology

The culture of digital resistance 103

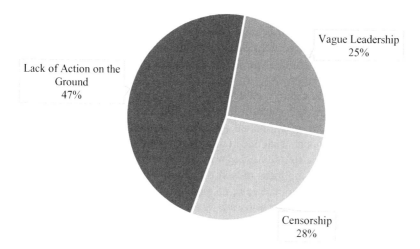

Figure 5.5 Biggest hindrance of communication technology

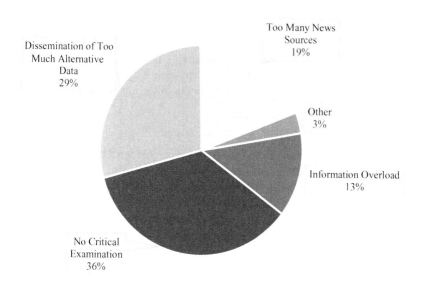

Figure 5.6 Drawbacks of access to unlimited information

This was evident in the many rallies that took place between 2012 and 2013 in India. Rather than engaging with the people through diplomatic dialogue and acknowledging their concerns about the inefficiencies of their system, the Indian government used water cannons, tear gas, and *lathi* (baton) charges to force them to disperse.[15] Fortunately, activists returned stronger and in greater numbers.

Movements abetted by technology also tend to lack structural hierarchy. While anonymity and vague leadership might help in particular circumstances, it also limns an internal instability that could be used to quickly topple the movement. That uncertainty is only likely to disappear if activists online manage to unify enough to agree upon an overarching goal or mission. Cohesive political movements form when previously unorganized groups find a political voice as vague dissatisfactions crystallize into a demand for change.[16] Following the *Nirbhaya* rape case, protestors—local and international, male and female—went out and demanded justice, heightened security, reliable public transport, and improved procedures surrounding sexual assault cases in India.

5.3 Changes to the definition of rape and rape laws in India

Prior to 2013, Section 375 of the Indian Penal Code (IPC) legally defined rape as penile penetration into the vagina, thereby making it a gender-specific crime.[17] This definition was revised through the Criminal Law (Amendment) Act of 2013, also known as the *Nirbhaya* Act, to include penile penetration of other orifices, object penetration, mouth contact with orifices, and the manipulation of a woman's body to cause penetration (Yardley & Bagri, 2018). A man is said to commit rape only if any of the aforementioned acts are committed under the following circumstances:

- Against her will
- Without her consent
- With her consent, when her consent has been obtained by putting her or any person known to her, in fear of death or of harm
- With her consent, when the man knows that he is not her husband
- With her consent when, at the time of giving consent, by reason of unsoundness of mind, intoxication, or the administration by him or through another of any stupefying substance, she is unable to understand the nature of that to which she gives consent
- With or without her consent, when she is under 18 years of age
- When she is unable to communicate consent

Despite legal expansions to the definition of rape, it is still officially recognized as a gender-specific crime. Males are the perpetrators, while females are the victims (Basu, 2007). This is evident in the annual crime statistics reports published by India's National Crime Records Bureau (NCRB), which contains a section titled "Crimes Against Women." The section provides detailed tables of quantitative data for several categories of crimes, including various types of sexual violence. Men don't have a similar section. Ultimately, this gives women the maneuverability to commit the crimes that they seek safety against to men. The lack of clauses concerning male rape may also sustain false notions that men cannot be sexually assaulted, particularly by women.

The *Nirbhaya* Act placed a considerable amount of emphasis on retribution in the form of harsher punishments for sex crimes, including longer prison sentences (seven years minimum for rape, although this was changed to ten years in 2018), with the possibility of life in prison (Mehta, 2013). A sentence of no less than 20 years was required for those found guilty of gang rape or causing injuries severe enough that the victim entered a permanent vegetative state. Those convicted of the former were also required to provide compensation to the victim for rehabilitation and medical expenses. Additionally, the amendment emphasized the potential enforcement of the death penalty for repeat offenders. Whether these harsher punishments have acted as a significant deterrent or exacerbated the issue by causing men to go out of their way to permanently silence a woman after sexually violating them is challenging to measure. Other changes brought about by the *Nirbhaya* Act include: (1) additional clauses for common crimes experienced by women such as stalking, disrobing, acid violence, sexual harassment, voyeurism, trafficking of persons, and insulting a woman's modesty; (2) mandatory first aid from government and private hospitals for rape victims; and (3) an increase in the age of consent from 16 to 18, so men accused of any form of sexual conduct with a woman under 18, regardless of consent, would constitute statutory rape. A notable exception not included in the *Nirbhaya* Act is marital rape. If the wife of a man is over 15, then any sexual act committed while the two are living together is not considered rape, although it could possibly be considered an act of domestic violence under other sections of the IPC. This clause may contribute to the maintenance of common rape myths related to the impossibility of raping (or being raped by) one's spouse.

5.4 Rape myths, women's status, and the gender ratio

Rape myths are attitudes and generally false beliefs about rape that are widely and persistently held and that serve to deny and justify male sexual aggression against women.[18] These myths find their roots in various cultural stereotypes. While most reported incidents do not coincide with rape myths, those that do, tend to receive national attention from major news outlets, possibly reinforcing the false impression that they occur more frequently: the belief that sexual assaults are crimes only committed by unfamiliar persons, for example. Delhi police statistics from 2012 revealed that 96% of those accused of rape were acquaintances or related to the victims, while only 3.68% were strangers.[19] In 2016, the number has seen little change. The NCRB reported that 94% of those accused were known to the victim. This widespread belief that rape is a "stranger crime" may leave many adults and children vulnerable (Chapleau & Oswald, 2010).

Research has shown that people often hold rape victims as somewhat responsible for their assault, irrespective of their gender or sexual orientation.[20] While most rape myths for men and women differ—with the former having more to do with the loss of masculinity or the total denial of the possibility of male rape occurring—many do believe that they exist and that some myths occur fairly regularly in society (Chennells, 2009). Common rape myths for women include women routinely lying about rape, women secretly wanting to be raped, and women "asking for sex" by dressing provocatively, or by being out late at night with a man (Larsen & Long, 1988). Figure 5.7 is based on a survey conducted on a random sample in India. Individuals were asked which rape myths they were most familiar with, thus providing us with an estimate of how pervasive these notions are in a given community.

As shown in the BBC documentary, *India's Daughter*, two of the defense lawyers—A. P. Singh and M. L. Sharma—who were involved in the

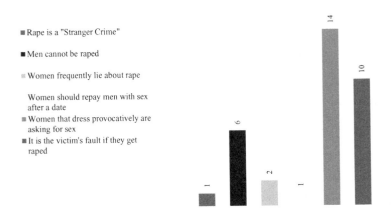

Figure 5.7 Most common rape myths

Nirbhaya case applied these myths in their responses during interviews in order to persuade viewers that their defendants were innocent. The following lines are excerpts from the documentary:

A. P. Singh: The girl (Jyoti) was with some unknown boy out on a date. In our society we never allow our girls to come out from the house after 6:30, 7:30, or 8:30 in the evening with any unknown person. . . . [S]he should not be put out on the street like food.

M. L. Sharma: If it's necessary that she go outside, she should go with her family members like father, mother, uncle, grandfather, grandmother, etc. She should not go out during night hours with her boyfriend.

Mukesh Singh, the interviewed rapist in the documentary, was shown saying that "*A decent girl won't roam around at 9 o'clock at night. A girl is far more responsible for rape than a boy. Boys and girls are not equal.*" He even stated that they raped Jyoti and beat Awindra because they thought that if they wronged them, then they wouldn't tell anyone. That, out of shame from what was done to them, they'd learn their lesson. Mukesh, A.P. Singh, and Sharma's comments highlight three critical subjects: established rape myths in India (as well as other countries), the status of Indian women in relation to men, and how some men perceive women.

Sheila Dixit, the Delhi chief minister from 1998 to 2013, explained in the BBC documentary, "*Many people in our society grow up thinking that girls are less important than boys, and because she's less important, you can do what you like with her.*" In India, women's positions are far more variable than in Western countries. Their status depends largely on their caste and class. Structural factors related to the social locations of men and women can "contribute to sexual violence and have an impact on women's ability to access the criminal justice system."[21] Often, it is women from working-class backgrounds or lower-caste groups that are the most vulnerable, especially from upper-caste men.[22] However, research has likewise shown that a large percentage of violent crime is committed by young, unmarried, low-status males.[23] Hence, demographics also play a role in disparity between the sexes.

Over half of India's population is under 25, and female infanticide and neglect are common in India, where men are seen as more valuable than girls.[24] Sex-selection practices distort the sex ratio, ultimately contributing to gender inequality. Table 5.1 shows the distribution of population for men and women in different states and union territories in India (Office of the Registrar General & Census Commissioner, 2011).

Table 5.1 Distribution of population for men and women in India (2011)

State/*union territory	Total population	Males	Females	Sex ratio
India	1,210,193,422	623,724,248	586,469,174	940
Jammu & Kashmir	12,548,926	6,665,561	5,883,365	883
Himachal Pradesh	6,856,509	3,473,892	3,382,617	974
Punjab	27,704,236	14,634,819	13,069,417	893
*Chandigarh	1,054,686	580,282	474,404	818
Uttarakhand	10,116,752	5,154,178	4,962,574	963
Haryana	25,353,081	13,505,130	11,847,951	877
*NCT of Delhi	16,753,235	8,976,410	7,776,825	866
Rajasthan	68,621,012	35,620,086	33,000,926	926
Uttar Pradesh	199,581,477	104,596,415	94,985,062	908
Bihar	103,804,637	54,185,347	49,619,290	916
Sikkim	607,688	321,661	286,027	889
Arunachal Pradesh	1,382,611	720,232	662,379	920
Nagaland	1,980,602	1,025,707	954,895	931
Manipur	2,721,756	1,369,764	1,351,992	987
Mizoram	1,091,014	552,339	538,675	975
Tripura	3,671,032	1,871,867	1,799,165	961
Meghalaya	2,964,007	1,492,668	1,471,339	986
Assam	31,169,272	15,954,927	15,214,345	954
West Bengal	91,347,736	46,927,389	44,420,347	947
Jharkhand	32,966,238	16,931,688	16,034,550	947
Orissa	41,947,358	21,201,678	20,745,680	978
Chhattisgarh	25,540,196	12,827,915	12,712,281	991
Madhya Pradesh	72,597,565	37,612,920	34,984,645	930
Gujarat	60,383,628	31,482,282	28,901,346	918
*Daman & Diu	242,911	150,100	92,811	618
*Dadra & Nagar Haveli	342,853	193,178	149,675	775
Maharashtra	112,372,972	58,361,397	54,011,575	925
Andhra Pradesh	84,665,533	42,509,881	42,155,652	992
Karnataka	61,130,704	31,057,742	30,072,962	968
Goa	1,457,723	740,711	717,012	968
*Lakshadweep	64,429	33,106	31,323	946
Kerala	33,387,677	16,021,290	17,366,387	1,084
Tamil Nadu	72,138,958	36,158,871	35,980,087	995
*Puducherry	1,244,464	610,485	633,979	1,038
Andaman & Nicobar Islands	379,944	202,330	177,614	878

Source: Provisional Population Totals of India, Paper 01, 2011 (Census of India).

The "Sex ratio" column in Table 5.1 refers to the number of females per 1,000 males. This varies across states and union territories. Only two, Kerala and Puducherry, have over 1,000 females. Daman and Diu, a single union territory comprising two separate regions, has the lowest sex ratio with only 618 females for every 1,000 males. Startling differences between the number of men and women can be the cause for significant security risks to society. It is also worth noting that this table does not take age into account, which would be relevant in the context of sex crimes.

Hudson and Boer in their article, "A Surplus of Men, a Deficit of Peace: Security and Sex Ratio's in Asia's Largest States," refer to the excess number of males that result from sex-selection practices as *"surplus males."* These men are essentially affected by a marriage squeeze, where marrying isn't an option because there aren't enough women to marry. In such cases, the characteristics of these surplus males are generally predictable—they likely come from the lowest socioeconomic class, are underemployed or unemployed, have nomadic lifestyles, and so on. Hudson and Boer further state that "compared with other males in society, surplus males are prone to seeking satisfaction through vice and violence and seek to capture resources that allow them to compete on a more equal footing with others." All this underscores a relationship between privilege, power, and sex that contribute to the protraction of women's supposed inferiority and rape myths, particularly those related to expectations that a woman must repay a man with intercourse; false beliefs that there are certain women that deserve sexual assault because of misinterpreted signals of consent or the unexamined acceptance that men are simply less inclined, if not entirely unable, to control their sexual urges, which of course is not the case.

Figures 5.8 and 5.9 breakdown what individuals consider to be the root causes of a skewed sex ratio in India as well as which consequence they believe needs to be addressed first. A majority of them cite societal beliefs as the underlying cause and gender inequality as the primary outcome that requires a solution.

Rape is a pervasive issue in many societies. While there has been an increasing trend for women to report sexual assault in several countries around the globe, it continues to prove challenging to measure. No single method or data source can accurately gauge the full extent of rape or other forms of sexual violence within a society because public discussion of these experiences is often confronted with distrust and insensitivity. In fact, one of the most common obstructions in addressing sex crimes is a lack of reporting by the victim. Holly Johnson, in an article regarding the limitations of a criminal justice response against sexual assault, wrote:

> The true incidence of sexual violence in women's lives will likely never be known. The stigma, shame, and blame associated with sexual violence have cast a shroud of silence over women's experiences and affect their willingness to report to police or to disclose to other public agencies.[25]

According to the Rape, Abuse, & Incest National Network (RAINN), about three out of four cases of sexual assault go unreported in the United States. This is due to several universal reasons such as the fear of retribution,

110 *Nalanda Roy & Stephanie Mae-Pedron*

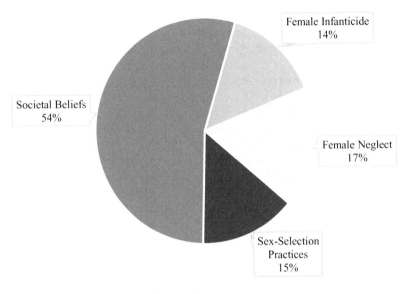

Figure 5.8 Causes of a skewed sex ratio

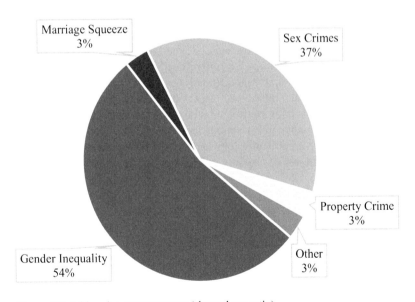

Figure 5.9 Addressing consequences (skewed sex ratio)

The culture of digital resistance 111

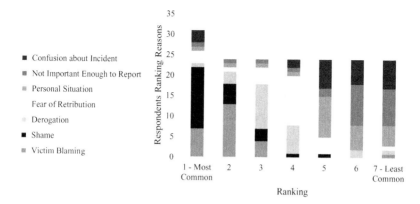

Figure 5.10 Ranking of reasons for unreported sex crimes

derogation, victim blaming, belief that the matter was a personal situation or unimportant, and so on. Figure 5.10 presents survey data that asked a random sample of individuals to rank seven possible reasons for the non-reporting of sex crimes from most to least common.

Reporting rape also goes against traditional societal norms, especially in India, where the number of unreported cases may be even higher than what was recorded by RAINN for the United States, owing to their divergent cultural views and customs. It is clear, however, that the prevalence of rape myths is harmful to society. They contribute to people's fear of reporting sex crimes and possibly even the misperception of certain situations. An individual may feel confused or may even overlook an incident of sexual assault because what happened to them might not have conformed to media portrayals of it. Evidence also suggests that individuals who believe in rape myths "are less likely to be empathetic or to report the incident to police and are more likely to attribute blame to victims and recommend lenient penalties."[26] Moreover, deep-seated negative views can prove detrimental to law enforcement agencies and jurors because their biases could overshadow the actual facts of a case.

Adequately addressing the issue of rape requires more than statewide action plans, the formation of special committees, or even the implementation of new legislation; it necessitates a fundamental shift in how women are perceived—and how women should perceive themselves—within a given society. If they are persistently talked down to within their communities and seen by others as subordinate, then conditions won't improve.

The *Nirbhaya* case is significant because it acted as a bridge for Indian citizens to bring the hardships constantly faced by women out into the open; it allowed them to publicly express their dissatisfaction on a massive scale. Open and reciprocal dialogue is the first step toward social change. After *Nirbhaya*, politicians acknowledged the public's concerns and endeavored to address them.

5.4 Nonviolent resistance: the theory of power

The *Nirbhaya* case was momentous not only for India, but also for social activists around the globe who promote peaceful uprisings to instigate social change. As stated earlier, sexual assault laws and broader public discourse concerning rape changed in India following significant online and in-person protests across the country. Civil resistance has its roots in individual ethics, diverse customs, and a powerful sense of person-by-person responsibility. The *Nirbhaya* incident, although one of its kind, is not the only instance of nonviolent action. Examples of the use of such approaches can be found all throughout history, such as Gandhi's Salt March (1930) following a law imposed by the British that Indians could not gather or sell salt within the country; the 1913 Women's Suffrage Parade in Washington, DC, that called for equal opportunity at the ballot box; and the Hungarians who engaged in nonviolent resistance against Austrian rule between the 1850s and the 1860s.[27] These groups, along with a spattering of others over the centuries, adopted different methods of civil protest to promote social change whether they were consciously aware of it or not.

Like other forms of resistance, nonviolent resistance stems from the basic power imbalance between a state government and its subjects, particularly if the subjects have been oppressed in a significant way over a prolonged period of time. Public unrest is fueled by an array of complex motives typically rooted in a state's history, such as an unquenchable desire for freedom, religious practices, national identity, basic human rights, and so on. These aims can intersect in significant ways, ultimately giving rise to a movement of people who seek to challenge the perceived source of their oppression. The underlying reason behind these motives can be boiled down to the shedding of false consciousness by the activists involved. They come to the straightforward realization that the ruling power's use of oppressive systems is not a sign of their strength over the masses, but a sign of their weakness.[28] It is a sign of an unreasonable fear by the elites that they will one day be toppled. Repressive tactics are often a disproportionate use of authority used to keep the broader society in line and, subsequently, the elites in power. Citizens, however, have the unique ability to turn the tide of power against the ruling class in their society. Owing to their numbers, they can harness the capabilities of a regime for their own purposes to better the conditions of the masses. This, however, requires a widespread understanding (from the general public) of their own subjugation, the impact of structural class dynamics and power legitimacy on their daily lives, and a realization that institutional change is a time-consuming process that will not happen overnight.

The world's leading theoretician on nonviolent action, Gene Sharp (1973), uses a theory of power based on the separation between rulers and their subjects. He posits that the power of rulers is derived from the consent of their subjects.[29] Should that consent be withdrawn, then a ruler's right to govern is reduced. Therefore, nonviolent resistance is the steady progression of the people's diminishing consent; it is a method used by the masses to challenge crucial societal issues such as human rights violations, genocide, authoritarianism, repressive legislation, summary arrests, and other forms of persecution. According to Kurt Schock, "[V]arious issue-related social movements have been almost exclusively nonviolent."[30] He cites women's movements, which not only encourages peaceful actions and relations, but also critiques the usage of violence. Labor movements have also depended on nonviolent methods classified by Gene Sharp to fight against exploitative industries. However, it is important to take into account the reality that when a state's legitimacy is defied (peacefully or otherwise), they often respond in a disparate manner that stirs more civil strife. This increased turbulence has the capacity to evolve into violent acts, especially by radicalized segments of the population directly affected by the government's actions (Martin, 2013). Sharp's theory of power is not without its shortcomings; it fails to consider many of the underlying structures that shape society. It also raises the issue of the meaningfulness of consent and its relevance to certain institutions. In other words, if legitimacy is derived from the assent of the governed, then would that assent still be regarded as vital if it is not informed?

Regardless of its drawbacks, Sharp's theory remains crucial because it suggests that physical force is merely an instrument, not the crux, of power. In certain situations, the use of violence by the public is entirely unnecessary for social change. If an ample part of the masses refuses to engage in actions that support the ruling class for a sufficient amount of time, then it is possible to undermine the power of the elites to the point of elimination.[31] Before delving deeper into Sharp's theory and the people's faculty to instill change, an understanding of power is necessary in order to effectively contest it. The organization of society necessitates the existence of bodies that regulate and enforce a system of formulated laws meant to coordinate the activities of the masses. These bodies or institutions inherently wield a form of political power because of their capacity to directly or indirectly influence the behavior of entire groups of people in the name of a larger—often political—objective.[32] Hence, political power may be regarded as the ability of an individual or institution to apply pressure onto people for the purpose of achieving or impeding a political goal.

When it comes to small-scale struggles, there is a tacit understanding that if enough individuals adopt the same practices, then it will result in widespread change: for example, the minute Paris uprisings in the first half of the 1800s. Unlike organized campaigns, the primary motivator in such protests is the morality of the individuals involved. Errol Harris argues that morality and power in political actions must go hand in hand. He further stated that the two concepts "must be so united that they become two aspects of the same social phenomenon," or else the government loses its legitimacy and becomes autocratic as a result.[33] An individual's morality, however, is dependent on many tangible and intangible factors, which are further complicated by the inclusion of a higher, transformative objective once enough participants are involved in the struggle. Sharp takes a different approach by emphasizing mostly exogenous variables. His theory of power is based on the fundamental view that legitimate power is derived from several sources in society. It is fragile because of its dependence on many groups for reinforcement (Sharp, 1973). One of the sources that Sharp underscores is human resources or people. This has several connotations. First, power is susceptible to the fluctuating will of the masses, so serving the needs of the majority is necessary, although that is not often the case in totalitarian regimes. This leads to the second point. That is, without some degree of consent by those governed, political power cannot be exercised. The existence of divisions within the general public—those who support the status quo and those who do not—can put a hamper on uprisings. Without the backing of the former, then social change is more difficult to achieve. Finally, political power can be controlled if the majority of the population is restrained in a significant way. In other words, power is reliant on the state's ability to enforce rules and the broad, communal obedience of citizens. The latter is considered by Sharp to be the heart of political power.

Obedience and command work in tandem with one another. Ruling individuals and institutions are dependent on the active or passive acquiescence of subordinate members (or subjects) to carry out the day-to-day operations that keep the rest of society functioning. These explicit and implicit directives, however, are not automatically followed by the masses; obedience differs with the person and is fundamentally voluntary. Positive and negative sanctions exist to ensure cooperation. Subjects, therefore, conform because of their own self-interest or a fear of sanctions.[34] Other reasons for obedience outlined by Sharp include force of habit, personal identification

The culture of digital resistance 115

with the ruler, indifference, absence of self-confidence among subjects, and moral obligation. Part of a regime's power lies in its ability to make individuals obey without them withdrawing their assent to the regime's right to rule over them. As previously discussed, consent is a fundamental aspect of Sharp's theory of power; political clout cannot be exercised without the subject's volition. Hence, every reason for a subject's obedience requires some form of personal approval to what's happening. The degree of approval is reliant on a range of external and internal forces. It varies over time as a consequence.

Sharp's theory of power—with its intense emphasis on the ruler-subject dynamic—does not encompass the range of structured systems within society.[35] He has, nevertheless, successfully organized a relevant portion of the field of peace studies in three key ways: (1) crafted a systematic framework for understanding the processes involved in civil struggles; (2) classified 198 methods of nonviolent action, including examples, into three main categories—noncooperation, nonviolent intervention, and protest and persuasion—thereby creating some semblance of order in the array of literature produced by scholars over the decades (refer to Appendix A for an overview of these methods); and (3) provided a set of conceptual tools and special processes for actionists to deal with repression.

One of these processes is political jiu-jitsu, which involves turning a regime's oppressive strength against it.[36] This does not function in all nonviolent struggles. According to Sharp, political jiu-jitsu works when actionists combine "nonviolent discipline with solidarity and persistence . . . [causing] the violence of the opponent's repression to be exposed in the worst possible light." When threatened, adversaries who hold more power often respond in a disproportionate manner. But atrocities committed against plainly nonviolent groups can greatly shift public opinion because of the opponent's typical inability to justify their actions. Eventually, this leads to power dynamics also shifting to the advantage of the nonviolent group. When tackling oppression, adopting a strategic approach is necessary. The selection and overall effectiveness of nonviolent methods (those identified by Sharp as well as additional methods conceived since) are dependent on the distinct context of the situation. Certain technical expertise and qualities such as patience and perseverance must be embraced and subsequently passed onto activists across communities. Because the process of political jiu-jitsu involves learning and honing a variety of soft skills, it is not bound by geographic borders. Accordingly, instances of its use can be found in various nation-states over the centuries. The 2012 Delhi gang rape can also be considered an example of people employing the power of political jiu-jitsu. The massive protests sparked by Jyoti's assault forced the Indian government to adopt new systems that work to protect women's rights. It also altered women's perceptions of sexual violence and traditional notions regarding where they stand in society by bringing international media attention to the pervasiveness of sex crimes in India.

Preparation is central to battling oppression; it helps individuals manage their anxieties and maintain their resolve in the face of antagonistic actions.[37] Participants in civil movements need to be mentally and physically prepared for the trials that they will face, especially if their oppressors react with aggression. Consistently publicizing these hostile responses, rather than reacting in a similar manner, is also imperative. Schock refers to the "adherence to nonviolent methods of action regardless of the actions of opponents"[38] as *nonviolent discipline*. It engages sympathizers and paves the path for more active, future participation. This, however, requires a certain degree of fortitude and the consideration of other variables. Fortunately, the ease of disseminating information in today's globalized world may contribute to an easier adherence to civil methods because of the immediate responses of support for those involved, although it is also important to take into account the amount of information consumed by people on a daily basis, which provides additional challenges to promulgating information through modern methods of communication such as those discussed earlier.

Shifting from methods of nonviolence to violence is relatively easy; this rings particularly clear if oppressors choose to adopt hostile practices. Civil resistance, then, requires a sense of perpetual awareness, so that the ideologies driving those involved are not twisted for the purpose of conflict escalation. According to Sharp's theory of power, it is also necessary for the public to display widespread withdrawal of their consent through nonviolent methods—as they did in the demonstrations that followed the *Nirbhaya* incident (Sharp, 2013). By doing so, citizens can challenge the political power of the ruling class. While some may do so for the sake of complete reconstruction of the current system, others may organize movements out of a more conservative desire for novel social reform programs and legislation that directly address their concerns. However, the efficiency of those programs and whether they remain in place is dependent on a multitude of other cultural and societal elements that should be considered upon their implementation in order for change to last.

5.5 National Crime Records Bureau statistics

Delhi experienced a trend of decreasing rape reports from 2005 to 2009, which was ended by a relatively marginal 8.10% (38 cases) increase in 2010. However, in the year after the *Nirbhaya* incident, Delhi experienced an overwhelming 171.73% (930 cases) report increase.

Note that while convicted case data hasn't varied significantly, data related to the number of persons convicted has remained relatively steady with the number of cases reported. In certain instances, as shown in the years 2013 and 2014, the number of persons convicted even exceeded the number of cases reported. This suggests high incidences of collaboration, gang rape, and/or stunted processing times for pending rape cases from previous years.

In India, an estimated 106 rapes were recorded per day in 2016.[39] That is more than double what was recorded just a decade prior. While a lack of recent crime statistics from the NCRB makes it difficult to determine whether or not registered cases have increased or decreased since 2016, statistics that date prior to that year—prior to the 2012 Delhi gang rape even—show a steady rise in the number of registered cases. That, along with a 2018 poll conducted by the Thomas Reuters Foundation, which dubbed India as the most dangerous country in the world for women, suggests that the rape epidemic is still at large, despite the 2013 changes to Indian laws. Although the number of reported rape cases dropped in 2015, the 12.4% spike that followed indicated only a momentary trend. According to the 2015 NCRB report, that year also saw an increase in other sexual offences against women such as disrobing, stalking, cruelty by relatives, and so on. Delhi, notably, didn't contribute to the 2015 drop as shown in Figure 5.11.

Figure 5.13 shows that conviction rates for reported rape cases have remained relatively steady since 2005, despite the action plans enacted by several states as well as the changes that the government made to Indian sexual assault laws in an attempt to address the issue. Conviction rates are

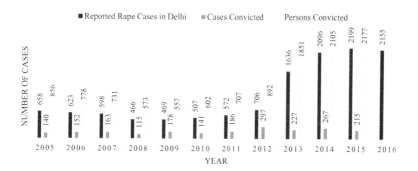

Figure 5.11 Registered rape cases, cases convicted, and persons convicted for rape in Delhi (2005–2016)

*Note the following: (1) 2016 currently has no recorded data for the number of cases and persons convicted for rape in Delhi; (2) information related to cases and persons convicted for rape in Delhi include pending case data from prior years.

about 25% with slight variation, which translates to roughly one in four convictions. According to the NCRB, the northeastern region typically boasts the highest conviction rates. In 2016, the NCRB also reported that 18,792 out of 38,947 total rape cases were disposed of by the police and courts and that 16,124 rape cases from 2015 were still pending investigation. For all crimes against women, the number of pending cases in 2016 was over 160,000.

In an attempt to ease the large backlog of pending rape cases and the growing number of registered rape cases from recent years, the Indian government created fast-track courts. Although they were meant to expedite the process, "proceedings have been bogged down by long waits for forensic evidence, police reports, and repeated adjournments. . . . [A]ccording to an amendment in Indian rape law, cases must be heard daily and be concluded within two months after charges are filed."[40] While the severe sentences outlined in the *Nirbhaya* Act may act as a deterrent, the relatively steady conviction rate in India over the last decade for those accused of rape highlights a crucial issue possibly related to how these cases are handled by authorities. That cases must be concluded within a specific—and relatively short two to six month—time frame might also contribute to the high number of registered rape cases disposed of by the courts.

It is possible that the sudden pressure on the Indian government to address concerns pertaining to sexual violence after *Nirbhaya* didn't afford them adequate time to fix the inefficiencies in their judicial system, before they implemented new legislation and individual state action plans. The

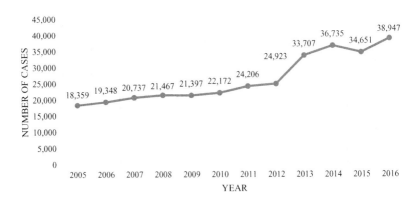

Figure 5.12 Registered rape cases by women in India (2005–2016)

*Note: The number of registered rape cases per year does not include pending case data from prior years.

The culture of digital resistance 119

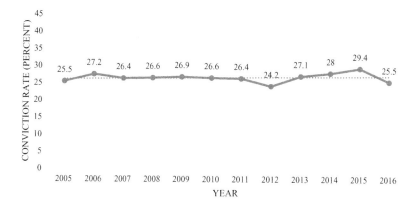

Figure 5.13 Conviction rate for registered rape cases by women in India (2005–2016)

prevalence of rape myths might also play a role in lagging conviction rates. Furthermore, knowledge of the exceedingly high number of rape cases thrown out by authorities (as shown in annual NCRB reports) might also reinforce false perceptions that most women lie about rape. While cases of false reports do exist, it is not as rife as some might believe. According to the National Sexual Violence Resource Center, in the United States, false reports constitute only 2%–10% of all cases reported.

Nonetheless, the 35% spike in reported rape cases by women immediately after 2012, as shown in Figure 5.12, and the continuous rise, in spite of lagging conviction rates and a backlog of pending rape cases, shows a positive, fundamental change in the perceptions of women toward reporting sexual crimes committed against them. Thus, the surge in reports is credited to an increase in women's confidence, which can be attributed to several factors: (1) the media's in-depth coverage of the case, including their humanitarian portrayal of it; (2) the feeling of solidarity felt by Indian women from activists across the globe who were able to relate to their plight through social media and other online modes of communication, specifically WhatsApp; (3) the public's enhanced information network, courtesy of the internet and modern communication technology, which enabled them to engage more openly with vital social issues related to gender inequality and justice.

A final consideration is that the case may have impacted the general public's perception regarding which sex crimes should be given increased attention by the legal system. Figure 5.14 is based on survey data that

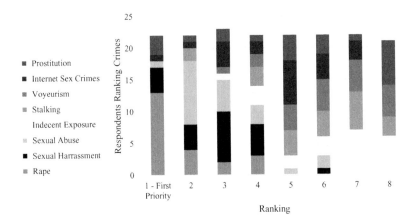

Figure 5.14 Ranking of sex crimes

specifically asked individuals to rank different sex crimes by the order that they felt the courts should prioritize them. Rape is, by far, considered the most important, with sexual abuse and sexual harassment trailing closely behind. Notably, voyeurism, indecent exposure, stalking, and prostitution all tend to rank on the lower end of the spectrum.

5.6 Conclusion

Today's digital media has the capacity to connect individuals from every corner of the globe. It provides a channel for them to learn about other cultures, connect with similar people, and participate in international social movements. Publicly voicing dissent about vital social dilemmas can spur unity, and eventually action, among large groups of people. This is the foundation for social change. The effects of such widespread opposition were witnessed during the months that followed the 2012 Delhi gang rape when several changes to Indian law were made as a direct result of the civil protests that dominated India after the incident. Men and women rallied to express their concerns regarding the safety of women and children in India. The scale of their support, as well as the openness with which they discussed the issue of rape, resulted in an attitudinal transformation among victims of sexual assault, which showed through an increase in reported sex crime data in subsequent years.

The intense outrage sparked by *Nirbhaya* changed women's perceptions of rape and, ultimately, paved the way for public discussion about

The culture of digital resistance 121

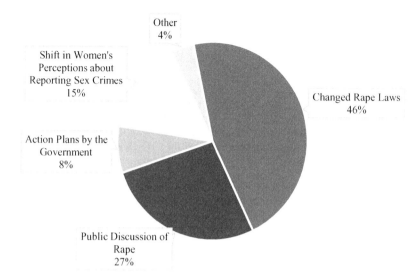

Figure 5.15 Most significant outcome of the *Nirbhaya* case

it. Experiences of sexual violence were no longer something to be hidden away for fear of derogation, victim blaming, or retribution, but announced, so that society could acknowledge it as an entrenched dilemma that required a remedy. Figure 5.15 shows what people believed to be the *Nirbhaya* case's most vital impact on Indian society.

But while the number of recorded rape cases increased as a result of this momentous case, low conviction rates and slow case processing times indicate other issues in India's judicial system that need to be addressed. Cultural norms related to the varying statuses of men and women as well as broader perceptions attached to victims of rape might also negatively affect the legal process.

Limitations of this study include a lack of Indian rape statistics related to men and an extensive focus on only a single subcategory of sex crimes. For succeeding analyses, breaking down each subcategory of sex crimes contained within "crimes against women" to examine which had the greatest spike in reports after 2013—and if they were able to maintain their numbers—would provide a more complete picture of the effects that the protests had after the *Nirbhaya* case. An exploration of the social factors that contributed to the 2015 dip in recorded cases as shown in Figure 5.12 might also unearth methods of combatting particular acts of sexual violence. Finally, examining which states in India had the highest number of sexual assault cases disposed of by the police and then measuring it against the number of reports received that year (including those still pending from previous years) may show interesting results possibly related to the prevalence of rape myths and their effect on India's legal system.

Notes

1 "Delhi gangrape victim's friend relives the horrifying 84 minutes of December 16 Night" *India Today* (September 13, 2013), accessed May 6, 2019, https://www.indiatoday.in/india/north/story/delhi-gangrape-victims-friend-relives-the-horrifying-84-minutes-of-december-16-night-210874-2013-09-13.
2 Nirbhaya case: "Four Indian men executed for 2012 Delhi bus rape and murder," *BBC.com* (March 2020), https://www.bbc.com/news/world-asia-india-51969961.
3 H. Al Adawy, "The spark of 'Nirbhaya:' Indian feminist interventions, common challenges, and prospects. Spotlight," (2017), http://www.irs.org.pk/spotlight-march-2014.pdf.
4 G. Bakshi, "The 'Nirbhaya' movement: An Indian feminist revolution," *Gnovis Journal* 17, no. 2 (2017): 43–55, https://repository.library.georgetown.edu/bitstream/handle/10822/1043685/Garima%20Bakshi.pdf.
5 G. Harris and H. Kumar, "Clashes break out in India at a protest over a rape case" (December 22, 2012), accessed May 6, 2019, https://www.nytimes.com/2012/12/23/world/asia/in-india-demonstrators-and-police-clash-at-protest-over-rape.html.
6 J. Dean, "Communicative capitalism: Circulation and the foreclosure of politics," *Cultural Politics* 1, no. 1 (2005): 51–74, https://commonconf.files.wordpress.com/2010/09/proofs-of-tech-fetish.pdf.
7 J. Friedland and K. Rogerson, "How political and social movements form on the internet and how they change over time," *Institute for Homeland Security Solutions* (2009), accessed April 30, 2019, https://sites.duke.edu/ihss/files/2011/12/IRW-Literature-Reviews-Political-and-Social-Movements.pdf.
8 Friedland and Rogerson, "How political and social movements form on the internet and how they change over time."
9 Bakshi, "The 'Nirbhaya' movement: An Indian feminist revolution."
10 R. Barn, "Social media and protest—the Indian Spring?" (September 9, 2013), https://www.huffingtonpost.co.uk/professor-ravinder-barn/india-social-media-and-protest_b_2430194.html
11 Dean, "Communicative capitalism: Circulation and the foreclosure of politics."
12 Dean, "Communicative capitalism: Circulation and the foreclosure of politics."
13 J. Dean, "Communicative capitalism and class struggle," *Spheres Journal for Digital Cultures*, 1, no. 1 (2014): 1–16.
14 M. Deuze and L. Ems, "Dissent at a distance," in R. Glas, S. Lammes, M. De Lange, J. Raessens, and I. De Vries (eds.), *The playful citizen: Civic engagement in a mediatized culture* (Amsterdam: Amsterdam University Press, 2019), 370–386, http://www.jstor.org/stable/j.ctvcmxpds.24.
15 Barn, "Social media and protest—the Indian Spring?"
16 A. William Gamson, *The strategy of social protest* (Wilmington, DE, USA: Wadsworth Pub Co, 1990).

17 G. Gangoli, "Controlling women's sexuality: Rape law in India," in G. Gangoli and N. Westmarland (eds.), *International approaches to rape* (Bristol, UK: Bristol University Press, 2011), 101–120.
18 K. A. Lonsway and L. F. Fitzgerald, "Rape myths," *Psychology of Women Quarterly* 18 (1994): 133–164, http://citeseerx.ist.psu.edu/viewdoc/download?doi=1 0.1.1.1012.5808&rep=rep1&type=pdf.
19 A. Pandey and T. Biswas, "Delhi witnessed over 700 rape cases in 2012, highest in last 10 years," (January 19, 2013), accessed May 6, 2019, https://www.ndtv.com/delhi-news/delhi-witnessed-over-700-rape-cases-in-2012-highest-in-last-10-years-510785.
20 D. Mitchell, R. Hirschman, and Gordon C. Nagayama Hall, "Attributions of victim responsibility, pleasure, and trauma in male rape," *The Journal of Sex Research* 36, no. 4 (1999): 369–373, http://www.jstor.org/stable/3813721.
21 M. Rew and G. Gangoli, "Continuities and change: The law commission and sexual violence," *Journal of Indian Law and Society*, 6 (2018): 110–124, https://research.birmingham.ac.uk/portal/files/39344168/article_16.08.16_final_Gangoli_Rew_clean_version_JILS_1_.pdf.
22 Gangoli, "Controlling women's sexuality: Rape law in India."
23 V. Hudson and A. D. Boer, "A surplus of men, a deficit of peace: Security and sex ratio's in Asia's largest states," *International Security* 26, no. 4 (2002): 5–38, https://docs.google.com/file/d/0B7NsBPUxnA4Mb1lGRmFUamNoenM/edit?pli=1.
24 G. Harris and H. Kumar, "Clashes break out in India at a protest over a rape case."
25 H. Johnson, "Limits of a criminal justice response: Trends in police and court processing of sexual assault," in E. Sheehy (ed.), *Sexual assault in Canada: Law, legal practice and women's activism* (Ottawa: University of Ottawa Press, 2012), 613–634, http://www.jstor.org/stable/j.ctt2jcb92.28.
26 H. Johnson, "Limits of a criminal justice response: Trends in police and court processing of sexual assault."
27 D. Cohen, "The day in history: The 1913 women's suffrage parade" (March 3, 2016), https://obamawhitehouse.archives.gov/blog/2016/03/03/this-day-history-1913-womens-suffrage-parade; T. Csapody and T. Weber, "Hungary: Nonviolent resistance against Austria, 1850s—1860s," in M. Bartkowski (ed.), *Recovering nonviolent history: Civil resistance in liberation struggles* (Boulder, CO: Lynne Rienner Publishers, 2012), 241–258; S. Graham, "Ghandi's salt march to Dandi" (1998), https://scholarblogs.emory.edu/postcolonialstudies/2014/06/20/gandhis-salt-march-to-dandi/; M. Werft and J. Ngalle, "5 peaceful protests that led to change" (July 8, 2016), https://www.globalcitizen.org/en/content/peace-protests-dallas-response/.
28 S. Popovic and M. Joksic, "The secret political Jiu-Jitsu" (March 3, 2014), https://foreignpolicy.com/2014/03/03/the-secret-of-political-jiu-jitsu/.
29 G. Sharp, *The politics of nonviolent action* (3 vols.) (Boston, MA: Porter Sargent Publishers, 1973).
30 K. Schock, "The practice and study of civil resistance," *Journal of Peace Research* 50, no. 3 (2013): 277–290. doi:10.1177/0022343313476530.
31 Schock, "The practice and study of civil resistance."
32 Sharp, *The politics of nonviolent action*.
33 E. Harris, "Political power," *Ethics* 68, no. 1 (1957): 1–10, http://www.jstor.org/stable/2379564.

34 Sharp, *The politics of nonviolent action*.
35 B. Martin, "Gene sharp's theory of power," *Journal of Peace Research* 26, no. 2 (1989): 213–222, http://www.jstor.org/stable/423870.
36 Popovic and Joksic, "The secret political Jiu-Jitsu."; Sharp, *The politics of nonviolent action*.
37 Popovic and Joksic, "The secret political Jiu-Jitsu."
38 Schock, "The practice and study of civil resistance."
39 C. Neeraj, "2016 saw 106 rapes a day, Delhi the capital here too" (n.d.), accessed April 30, 2019, https://epaper.timesgroup.com/Olive/ODN/TimesOfIndia/shared/ShowArticle.aspx?doc=TOIDEL%2F2017%2F12%2F01&entity=Ar02311&sk=1051FF23.
40 A. Gowen, "India now has nearly 400 fast-track courts for rape cases, but fast is a relative term," *Washington Post* (August 15, 2016), accessed May 7, 2019, https://www.washingtonpost.com/world/asia_pacific/india-has-nearly-400-fast-track-courts-for-rape-cases-but-fast-is-a-relative-term/2016/08/15/e57d44b8-54cc-11e6-bbf5-957ad17b4385_story.html.

References

Al Adawy, H. (2014). The spark of 'Nirbhaya:' Indian feminist interventions, common challenges, and prospects. *Spotlight*. http://irs.org.pk/spotlight-march-2014.pdf

Bakshi, G. (2017). The 'Nirbhaya' movement: An Indian feminist revolution. *Gnovis Journal*, 17(2), 43–55. https://repository.library.georgetown.edu/bitstream/handle/10822/1043685/Garima%20Bakshi.pdf?sequence=1&isAllowed=y

Barn, R. (2013, September 9). Social media and protest—The Indian spring? *Huffington Post*. https://www.huffingtonpost.co.uk/professor-ravinder-barn/india-social-media-and-protest_b_2430194.html?guccounter=1

Basu, K. (2007, July 25). India's demographic dividend. *BBC*. http://news.bbc.co.uk/2/hi/south_asia/6911544.stm

Chapleau, K., & Oswald, D. (2010). Power, sex, and rape myth acceptance: Testing two models of rape proclivity. *The Journal of Sex Research*, 47(1), 66–78. http://www.jstor.org/stable/25676437

Chennells, R. (2009). Sentencing: The "real rape" myth. *Agenda: Empowering Women for Gender Equity* (82), 23–38. http://www.jstor.org/stable/41321365

Cohen, D. (2016, March 3). The day in history: The 1913 women's suffrage parade. *The White House*. https://obamawhitehouse.archives.gov/blog/2016/03/03/this-day-history-1913-womens-suffrage-parade

Csapody, T., & Weber, T. (2012). Hungary: Nonviolent resistance against Austria, 1850s—1860s. In M. Bartkowski (Ed.), *Recovering nonviolent history: Civil resistance in liberation struggles* (pp. 241–258). Lynne Rienner Publishers.

Dean, J. (2005). Communicative capitalism: Circulation and the foreclosure of politics. *Cultural Politics*, 1(1), 51–74. https://commonconf.files.wordpress.com/2010/09/proofs-of-tech-fetish.pdf

Dean, J. (2014). Communicative capitalism and class struggle. *Spheres Journal for Digital Cultures, 1*(1), 1–16.
Deuze, M., & Ems, L. (2019). Dissent at a distance. In R. Glas, S. Lammes, M. De Lange, J. Raessens, & I. De Vries (Eds.), *The playful citizen: Civic engagement in a mediatized culture* (pp. 370–386). Amsterdam University Press. http://www.jstor.org/stable/j.ctvcmxpds.24
Friedland, J., & Rogerson, K. (2009). *How political and social movements form on the internet and how they change over time*. Institute for Homeland Security Solutions. https://sites.duke.edu/ihss/files/2011/12/IRW-Literature-Reviews-Political-and-Social-Movements.pdf
Gamson, W. A. (1990). *The strategy of social protest*. Wadsworth Pub Co.
Gangoli, G. (2011). Controlling women's sexuality: Rape law in India. In G. Gangoli & N. Westmarland (Eds.), *International approaches to rape* (pp. 101–120). Bristol University Press.
Gowen, A. (2016, August 15). India now has nearly 400 fast-track courts for rape cases, but fast is a relative term. *Washington Post*. https://www.washingtonpost.com/world/asia_pacific/india-has-nearly-400-fast-track-courts-for-rape-cases-but-fast-is-a-relative-term/2016/08/15/e57d44b8-54cc-11e6-bbf5-957ad17b4385_story.html?noredirect=on&utm_term=.43ae303313ca
Graham, S. (1998). Ghandi's salt march to Dandi. *Emory*. https://scholarblogs.emory.edu/postcolonialstudies/2014/06/20/gandhis-salt-march-to-dandi/
Harris, E. (1957). Political power. *Ethics, 68*(1), 1–10. http://www.jstor.org/stable/2379564.
Harris, G., & Kumar, H. (2012, December 22). Clashes break out in India at a protest over a rape case. *New York Times*. https://www.nytimes.com/2012/12/23/world/asia/in-india-demonstrators-and-police-clash-at-protest-over-rape.html
Hudson, V., & Boer, A.D. (2002). A surplus of men, a deficit of peace: Security and sex ratios in Asia's largest states. *International Security, 26*(4), 5–38. https://docs.google.com/file/d/0B7NsBPUxnA4Mb1lGRmFUamNoenM/edit?pli=1
India Today. (2013, September 13). *Delhi gangrape victim's friend relives the horrifying 84 minutes of December 16 night*. https://www.indiatoday.in/india/north/story/delhi-gangrape-victims-friend-relives-the-horrifying-84-minutes-of-december-16-night-210874-2013-09-13
Johnson, H. (2012). Limits of a criminal justice response: Trends in police and court processing of sexual assault. In E. Sheehy (Ed.), *Sexual assault in Canada: Law, legal practice and women's activism* (pp. 613–634). University of Ottawa Press. http://www.jstor.org/stable/j.ctt2jcb92.28
Larsen, K., & Long, E. (1988). Attitudes toward rape. *The Journal of Sex Research, 24*, 299–304. http://www.jstor.org/stable/3812852
Lonsway, K. A., & Fitzgerald, L. F. (1994). Rape myths. *Psychology of Women Quarterly, 18*, 133–164. http://citeseerx.ist.psu.edu/viewdoc/download?doi=10.1.1.1012.5808&rep=rep1&type=pdf

Martin, B. (1989). Gene Sharp's theory of power. *Journal of Peace Research, 26*(2), 213–222. http://www.jstor.org/stable/423870

Martin, B. (2013). The politics of Gene Sharp. *Ghandi Marg, 35*(2), 201–230.

Mehta, S. (2013). Rape law in India: Problems in prosecution due to loopholes in the law. *SSRN Electronic Journal*. https://doi.org/10.2139/ssrn.2250448

Mitchell, D., Hirschman, R., & Gordon C. Nagayama Hall. (1999). Attributions of victim responsibility, pleasure, and trauma in male rape. *The Journal of Sex Research, 36*(4), 369–373. http://www.jstor.org/stable/3813721

National Crime Records Bureau. (n.d.). Crime in India—All previous publications. *Ministry of Home Affairs*. https://ncrb.gov.in/en/crime-india

National Sexual Violence Resource Center. (n.d.). *Statistics*. https://www.nsvrc.org/statistics

Neeraj, C. (2017, December 1). 2016 saw 106 rapes a day, Delhi the capital here too. *The Times of India* https://epaper.timesgroup.com/Olive/ODN/TimesOfIndia/shared/ShowArticle.aspx?doc=TOIDEL%2F2017%2F12%2F01&entity=Ar02311&sk=1051FF23&mode=text

Office of the Registrar General & Census Commissioner. (2011). *Provisional population totals of India* (Paper 01, 2011). Ministry of Home Affairs. http://www.censusindia.gov.in/2011-prov-results/prov_results_paper1_india.html

Pandey, A., & Biswas, T. (2013, January 19). Delhi witness 700 rape cases in 2012, highest in 10 years. *NDTV*. https://www.ndtv.com/delhi-news/delhi-witnessed-over-700-rape-cases-in-2012-highest-in-last-10-years-510785

Popovic, S., & Joksic, M. (2014, March 3). The secret political jiu-jitsu. *Foreign Policy*. https://foreignpolicy.com/2014/03/03/the-secret-of-political-jiu-jitsu/

RAINN. (n.d.). *The criminal justice system: Statistics*. https://www.rainn.org/statistics/criminal-justice-system

Rew, M., & Gangoli, G. (2018). Continuities and change: The law commission and sexual violence. *Journal of Indian Law and Society, 6*, 110–124. https://research.birmingham.ac.uk/portal/files/39344168/article_16.08.16_final_Gangoli_Rew_clean_version_JILS_1_.pdf

Schock, K. (2013). The practice and study of civil resistance. *Journal of Peace Research, 50*(3), 277–290. doi:10.1177/0022343313476530

Sharp, G. (1973). *The politics of nonviolent action* (3 vols.). Porter Sargent Publishers.

Sharp, G. (2013). *How nonviolent struggle works*. The Albert Einstein Institution.

Thompson, R. (2011). Radicalization and the use of social media. *Journal of Strategic Security, 4*(4), 167–190. https://www.jstor.org/stable/26463917

Werft, M., & Ngalle, J. (2016, July 8). 5 peaceful protests that led to change. *Global Citizen*. https://www.globalcitizen.org/en/content/peace-protests-dallas-response/

Yardley, J., & Bagri, N. T. (2018, October 19). Notorious attack spurs India to approve new rape laws. *New York Times*. https://www.nytimes.com/2013/02/04/world/asia/india-approves-tougher-rape-laws.html

Appendix A

Table 5A.1 Gene Sharp's 198 methods of nonviolent action

Protest and persuasion	Noncooperation	Nonviolent intervention
Formal statements • Public speeches • Letters of opposition or support • Declarations by organizations and institutions • Signed public statements • Declarations of indictments and intentions • Group or mass petitions **Communications with a wider audience** • Slogans, caricatures, and symbols • Banners, posters, and displayed communications • Leaflets, pamphlets, and books	**Ostracism of persons** • Social boycott • Selective social boycott • Lysistratic nonaction • Excommunication • Interdict **Noncooperation with social events, customs, and institutions** • Suspension of social and sports activities • Boycott of social affairs • Student strike • Social disobedience • Withdrawal from social institutions **Withdrawal from the social system** • Stay-at-home • Total personal noncooperation • "Flight" of workers • Sanctuary • Collective disappearance • Protest emigration	**Rejection of authority** • Withholding or withdrawal of allegiance • Refusal of public support • Literature and speeches advocating resistance **Citizens' noncooperation with government** • Boycott of legislative bodies • Boycott of elections • Boycott of government employment and positions • Boycott of government departments, agencies, and other bodies • Withdrawal from government educational institutions • Boycott of government-supported organizations • Refusal of assistance to enforcement agents • Removal of own signs and placemarks • Refusal to accept appointed officials • Refusal to dissolve existing institutions **Citizens' alternatives to obedience** • Reluctant and slow compliance • Nonobedience in absence of direct supervision	**Psychological intervention** • Self-exposure to the elements • The fast (Fast of moral pressure; hunger strike; satyagrahic fast) • Reverse trial • Nonviolent harassment **Physical intervention** • Sit-in • Stand-in • Ride-in • Wade-in • Mill-in • Pray-in • Nonviolent raids • Nonviolent air raids • Nonviolent invasion • Nonviolent interjection • Nonviolent obstruction • Nonviolent occupation **Social intervention** • Establishing new social patterns • Overloading of facilities

The culture of digital resistance 129

- Newspapers and journals
- Records, radio, and television
- Skywriting and earth writing

Group representations
- Deputations
- Mock awards
- Group lobbying
- Picketing
- Mock elections

Symbolic public acts
- Displays of flags and symbolic colors
- Wearing of symbols
- Prayer and worship
- Delivering symbolic objects
- Protest disrobings

Actions by consumers
- Consumers' boycott
- Nonconsumption of boycotted goods
- Policy of austerity
- Rent withholding
- Refusal to rent
- National consumers' boycott
- International consumers' boycott

Action by workers and producers
- Workmen's boycott
- Producers' boycott

Action by middlemen

- Popular nonobedience
- Disguised disobedience
- Refusal of an assemblage or meeting to disperse
- Sit-down
- Noncooperation with conscription and deportation
- Hiding, escape, and false identities
- Civil disobedience of "illegitimate" laws

Action by government personnel
- Selective refusal of assistance by government aides
- Blocking of lines of command and information
- Stalling and obstruction

- Stall-in
- Speak-in
- Guerrilla theater
- Alternative social institutions
- Alternative communication system

Economic intervention
- Reverse strike
- Stay-in strike
- Nonviolent land seizure
- Defiance of blockades
- Politically motivated counterfeiting

(*Continued*)

Table 5A.1 (Continued)

Protest and persuasion	Noncooperation	Nonviolent intervention
• Destruction of own property • Symbolic lights • Displays of portraits • Paint as protest • New signs and names • Symbolic sounds • Symbolic reclamations • Rude gestures **Pressures on individuals** • "Haunting" officials • Taunting officials • Fraternization • Vigils **Drama and music** • Humorous skits and pranks • Performances of plays and music • Singing **Processions** • Marches • Parades	• Suppliers' and handlers' boycott **Action by owners and management** • Traders' boycott • Refusal to let or sell property • Lockout • Refusal of industrial assistance • Merchants' "general strike" **Action by holders of financial resources** • Withdrawal of bank deposits • Refusal to pay fees, dues, and assessments • Refusal to pay debts or interest • Severance of funds and credit • Revenue refusal • Refusal of a government's money • General administrative noncooperation • Judicial noncooperation • Deliberate inefficiency and selective noncooperation by enforcement agents • Mutiny **Domestic governmental action** • Quasi-legal evasions and delays • Noncooperation by constituent governmental units **International governmental action** • Changes in diplomatic and other representations • Delay and cancellation of diplomatic events • Withholding of diplomatic recognition • Severance of diplomatic relations • Withdrawal from international organizations • Refusal of membership in international bodies • Expulsion from international organizations	• Preclusive purchasing • Seizure of assets • Dumping • Selective patronage • Alternative markets • Alternative transportation systems • Alternative economic institutions **Political intervention** • Overloading of administrative systems • Disclosing identities of secret agents • Seeking imprisonment • Civil disobedience of "neutral" laws • Work on without collaboration • Dual sovereignty and parallel government

- Religious processions
- Pilgrimages
- Motorcades

Honoring the dead
- Political mourning
- Mock funerals
- Demonstrative funerals
- Homage at burial places

Public assemblies
- Assemblies of protest or support
- Protest meetings
- Camouflaged meetings of protest
- Teach-ins

Withdrawal and renunciation
- Walk-outs
- Silence
- Renouncing honors
- Turning one's back

Action by governments
- Domestic embargo
- Blacklisting of traders
- International sellers' embargo
- International buyers' embargo
- International trade embargo

Symbolic strikes
- Protest strike
- Quickie walkout (lightning strike)

Agricultural strikes
- Peasant strike
- Farm workers' strike

Strikes by special groups
- Refusal of impressed labor
- Prisoners' strike
- Craft strike
- Professional strike

(Continued)

Table 5A.1 (Continued)

Protest and persuasion	Noncooperation	Nonviolent intervention
	Ordinary industrial strikes • Establishment strike • Industry strike • Sympathetic strike **Restricted strikes** • Detailed strike • Bumper strike • Slowdown strike • Working-to-rule strike • Reporting "sick" (sick-in) • Strike by resignation • Limited strike • Selective strike **Multi-industry strikes** • Generalized strike • General strike **Combination of strikes and economic closures** • Hartal • Economic shutdown	

Source: Sharp, G. (1973). *The politics of nonviolent action* (3 vols.). Boston, MA: Porter Sargent Publishers.

6 Conclusion
Will civil resistance work?

Nalanda Roy

6.1 Will civil resistance work?

Nonviolent Resistances in the Contemporary World discusses an important question: What happens after a successful civil resistance movement?

Well, one thing we have learned is that, in politics, success is seldom permanent,[1] and a one-size-fits-all approach does not always work. I am often apprehensive of approaches that try to address this issue with tunnel vision. There are times when one has to exert pressure again in order to revert to a greater degree of respect for democracy.[2] A one-size-fits-all approach does not always work. I am often leery of approaches that try to address this issue with tunnel vision. The volume demonstrates that each case of nonviolent resistance is significantly different and that demonstrations, support, and other activities can take many different forms. The preconditions of a successful nonviolent struggle often include some form of civil society, the use of technology and social media, and even an existing electoral system. As Chenoweth writes, "[C]ountries in which there were nonviolent campaigns were about ten times likelier to transition to democracies within a five-year period compared to countries in which there were violent campaigns—whether the campaigns succeeded or failed."[3]

Each case study in this volume demonstrates that civil resistance campaigns can lead to long-term reforms. In fact, such resistance movements are more likely to bring about democratization than violent campaigns. For example, the Kefaya movement, also known as the Egyptian Movement for Change, was an indigenous movement for political reform organized in late 2004 in opposition to the regime of Egyptian president Hosni Mubarak. Members of the movement explored the challenges to grassroots organizing that has attempted to bring about democracy and implement political reform in the Arab world. Although the Kefaya movement failed in the short term, the experiences gathered during that movement surely created the groundwork to effectively organize the 2011 uprisings in Egypt.

DOI: 10.4324/9781003109310-6

It also inspired similar movements in Libya, where Khalas was formed to oppose Colonel Muammar al-Qaddafi's retention of power, or the movement in Sudan where more than 3,000 Sudanese gathered to oppose the government of Omar al-Bashir. In other words, the Kefaya movement demonstrated "no to a fifth term and no to hereditary rule."[4] In fact, their implicit challenge to a sitting regime earned Kefaya praise from both the international and the Arab world. Kefaya was initially successful, in part, because of its ability to exploit communication technology.[5] We saw a similar trend in the case of the *Nirbhaya* anti-rape movement in India where activists' ability to document and expose human rights abuses and violence against women forced the government to prosecute the perpetrators of these acts. Technology was used to share the "black dot of shame," and the symbol sparked questions in people's minds, paving the way for interested citizens to join active online protests against the government. In fact, the visibility of the case was greatly enhanced as users simultaneously shared messages of outrage and support across social media platforms like Facebook and Twitter.[6]

Similarly, the 2007 Saffron Revolution in Myanmar was brutally suppressed at the time, but it ultimately led to voluntary democratic reforms by the government by 2012. In Myanmar, a large-scale armed conflict led to the process of democratization in the country; however, it was accompanied by extreme violence against the Rohingya community. In fact, one needs to understand that such cases are exceptions rather than the norm. Besides, one should not assume that nonviolent campaigns will always lead to democracies. But one should remember, "a satyagrahi obeys the laws of society intelligently and of his own free will, because he considers it to be his sacred duty to do so. It is only when a person has thus obeyed the laws of society scrupulously that he is in a position to judge as to which particular rules are good and just and which are unjust and iniquitous."[7] Only then does the right accrue to him of the civil disobedience of certain laws in well-defined circumstances.

Sometimes, external support and support from other pro-democracy groups as well as international pressure on authoritarian regimes may prove to be beneficial. Through its media outlets, reformers can create a platform by publicly endorsing their efforts. Therefore, the media can play an "integral role in pressuring governments to tolerate reform efforts."[8] Such policies send a signal over time to both the regimes and populations that the international community values those who advocate for democracy. In fact, such actions could help protect such movements and individuals from repression and intimidation. For example, the Kefaya movement was inspired by similar movements like the Orange Revolution in Ukraine. At the same time, it also inspired others to follow in its footsteps.

Conclusion 135

Usually, nonviolent resistance may have a strategic advantage over violent resistance for several reasons.[9] In particular, repressing a nonviolent campaign may backfire. This is exactly what happened in India during the *Nirbhaya* movement, and it led to mass mobilization against the regime as well as international condemnation of the current administration. Further, nonviolent resistance campaigns can appear to be more open to negotiation and bargaining. Therefore, one can argue that nonviolent campaigns are more likely to succeed in the face of repression than are violent campaigns.

The intellectual significance of this edited volume is to educate the public, policymakers, and academics about the consequences of civil resistance and to improve understanding of concepts such as mobilization, resilience, and leverage, which are central to the dynamics of civil resistance. The primary objective of the volume is to provide an interesting analysis of a number of cases where political struggles against incumbent governments took a violent form and a number of cases where nonviolent methods were used. The volume seeks to explain whether nonviolent resistance has been adopted because the issue is perceived to be relatively easy or because the adversary is perceived to be weak. There are several questions that will need to be answered over time. More research is required to develop measures of mass mobilization, empirically assess the degree of unity in the nonviolent struggle, and to understand a variety of other relevant factors.

This book is extremely topical, and there are a few things that will make it a marketable resource for scholars and students eager to delve into issues of nonviolent resistance in the future. First, this volume is short, but succinct. Second, it emphasizes the concept of civil resistance and people power. These issues are highly relevant now because of recent events like the attack on the US Capitol, Me Too, the Women's March, Black Lives Matter, and others. Many of these events are unprecedented and could even be "the tip of the iceberg." As Martin Luther King once said, "[W]e adopt the means of nonviolence because our end is a community at peace with itself. We will try to persuade with our words, but if our words fail, we will try to persuade with our acts."[10]

The book can serve as an upper-level text in college courses. Human rights, nonviolent resistance, and conflict resolution are now widely taught and researched in tertiary education institutions, think tanks, and research institutes. Depending on the course, this volume could work as a primary text or as a supplementary text. If the course is largely theoretical, this volume can be used as a supplementary text. But if the course is empirical (focused on case studies) or theoretical/empirical combined, then it will be a very suitable primary text. In other words, a volume like this has a strong appeal for scholars, researchers, students, libraries, and practitioners across the world.

Notes

1 "Success is not final; failure is not fatal: it is the courage to continue that counts."-Winston Churchill, https://www.business-standard.com/content/specials/success-is-not-final-failure-is-not-fatal-it-is-the-courage-to-continue-that-counts-winston-churchill-121042300664_1.html. Accessed: November 10, 2021.
2 Erica Chenoweth and Maria J. Stephan. Why Civil Resistance Works: The Strategic Logic of Nonviolent Conflict, Columbia University Press, 2012.
3 Erica Chenoweth and Maria J. Stephan, *Why civil resistance works: The strategic logic of nonviolent conflict* (New York: Columbia University Press, 2012).
4 Gamal Essam El-Din, "Space to say 'no' to the president," *Al-Ahram Weekly* (December 2004). As of January 31, 2008, accessed April 27, 2021, http://weekly.ahram.org.eg/2004/721/eg4.htm.
5 N. Oweidat, C. Benard, D. Stahl, W. Kildani, E. O'Connell, and A. Grant, "Kefaya's successes," in The Kefaya movement: A case study of a grassroots reform initiative (Santa Monica, CA; Arlington, VA; and Pittsburgh, PA: RAND Corporation, 2018), 17–26, accessed April 27, 2021, http://www.jstor.org/stable/10.7249/mg778osd.8.
6 V. Ramani Chitra, "Black dot campaign goes viral," *The Hindu* (April 22, 2016), https://www.thehindu.com/news/cities/bangalore/black-dot-campaign-goes-viral/article6221711.ece.
7 Grover, D. C. (1977). SATYAGRAHA AND DEMOCRATIC POWER STRUCTURE. The Indian Journal of Political Science, 38(1), 10–29. http://www.jstor.org/stable/41854772.
8 N. Oweidat, C. Benard, D. Stahl, W. Kildani, E. O'Connell and A. Grant, "Kefaya's successes," 43–54.
9 Chenoweth, E. & Stephan, M.J. (2012). *Why civil resistance works: The strategic logic of nonviolent conflict.* Columbia University Press.
10 16 Martin Luther King quotes to remember, January 15, 2016, https://www.amnesty.org/en/latest/campaigns/2016/01/16-martin-luther-king-quotes-to-remember/.

References

Chenoweth, E., & Stephan, M. J. (2012). *Why civil resistance works: The strategic logic of nonviolent conflict.* Columbia University Press.
El-Din, G. E. (2004). *Space to Say 'No' to the President.* Al-Ahram Weekly. https://english.ahram.org.eg/Index.aspx
Oweidat, N., Benard, C., Stahl, D., Kildani, W., O'Connell, E., & Grant, A. (2008a). Kefaya's successes. In *The Kefaya movement: A case study of a grassroots reform initiative* (pp. 17–26). RAND Corporation. http://www.jstor.org/stable/10.7249/mg778osd.8
Oweidat, N., Benard, C., Stahl, D., Kildani, W., O'Connell, E., & Grant, A. (2008b). Kefaya's successes. In *The Kefaya movement: A case study of a grassroots reform initiative* (pp. 43–54). RAND Corporation. http://www.jstor.org/stable/10.7249/mg778osd.8

Index

AKIN (US-based Kurdish rights group) 4
AKP (*Adalet ve Kalkınma Partisi*) 4, 63–64, 66–68, 70–71, 79, 81–82; see also Erdoğan, Recep Tayyip
al-Bashir, Omar 136
Alexander I, Tzar of Russia 35
al-Qaddafi, Muammar 136
Arab Spring 2, 30
Atatürk, Kemal 62
Austrian Empire 39, 45

Badeni, Kazimierz 39
Black Lives Matter 2, 7–8, 137
Bobrzyński, Michal 55

capacity building 23
Chang, Peng-Chun 70
civil resistance 1; long-term reforms 135; objectives 8–12; popular campaigns 21
Civil Rights Movement 7
civil society, local 23
color revolutions 30
COVID-19 pandemic 8
cultural violence 13

Demirtaş, Selahattin 68, 79
direct violence 11–14, 16, 18
Drzymała, Michal 42, 56

Erdoğan, Recep Tayyip 64; democratized parliamentary system 66; EU membership 68; human right issues, support of 70; local elections 68; mass arrests and terrorism 81; military coups 67; Rojava territories 69; support for the Syrian Kurds 69; tweets on 79, 81
ethnic discrimination 12

Galtung, Johan 6–7; on structural and cultural violence 8, 12–16, 22–23; theory of violence 8
Gandhi, Mahatma 7; civil resistance movement 1; nonviolence movement 6; Salt March 114
Gülen, Fethullah 67

Habsburg monarchy 1
HDP (*Halkların Demokratik Partisi*): 2019 local elections 68; agenda-building role 74–77; Erdoğan's relationship with 67; Kurdish political parties and 64–67; Turkish media, blacklisting 71, 74–82

India: communication technology 99–106; digital resistance 99; National Crime Records Bureau statistics on rape 118–122; *Nirbhaya* Act 106–107, 120; *Nirbhaya* incident 98–102, 106–107, 109, 114, 118, 120, 122–123; nonviolent resistance 114–118; Rape, Abuse, & Incest National Network (RAINN) 111, 113; rape and rape laws 106–114; rape myths 107–109; sex/gender ratio 107–111; traditional societal norms 113

138 *Index*

indirect violence 14
international nongovernmental organizations (INGOs) 11

Kefaya movement 135–136
King, Martin Luther 6–7, 137
Konopnicka, Maria 42, 57
Kościuszko, Tadeusz 3, 32, 35, 41
Kurdish political party *see* HDP (*Halkların Demokratik Partisi*)
Kurdistan/Kurdish: geography 61; human rights issues 93–97; international power struggles 61; Islamic State (ISIS/ISIL) 69; Kurdish identity 61–62; Kurdistan Regional Government (KRG) 68; opposition media 61; PKK—Kurdistan Workers Party 62–64; PYD (Democratic Union Party) 69; Treaty of Sevre 61; YPG (Peoples Protection Units) 69

legal resistance movement 1
Lutz, Bertha 70

Malik, Charles 70
Mandela, Nelson 6
Mehta, Hansa 70
Me Too movement 2, 137
Mubarak, Hosni 135

Napoleon 35
Nationalist Movement Party (MHP) 81
Nirbhaya incident 98–102
nonviolence: cultural 18; direct 17; structural 18; *vs.* violence 16–18
nonviolent action: definition 17; inclusion in peace processes 24
nonviolent resistance: forms of contention 54; literature on 52; *see also specific countries*

Öcalan, Abdullah 79
Orange Revolution in Ukraine 136

peace processes: nonviolence and 19–21; societal level 23; socioeconomic spheres 23–24
Poland: 1907–1914 military planning 53; anti-Russian nationalism 43; Austro-Hungary alliance 39;

Battle of Ra cławice 41; Brest-Litowsk peace treaty 45; Catholics 42; collaboration and resistance context 36–37, 46; communist government 60; cross-class solidarity 41; denationalization 42; Galician autonomy 39–42, 45; German partition 39, 43–44, 46; Grand Duchy of Poznań 36; independence through violence 34, 44; Kościuszko uprising, failure of 35; longest war of modern Europe, historical series 58; nationalistic violence 41; nonviolent resistance 31–34, 47; patriotism 42; personal note from the author 59; post 1864 realities 37–38; Russian partition 38–39, 43–44, 46; St. Petersburg Convention of 1797 35; and Ukrainian nationalisms 40
police brutality 12
political actors 71–74, 81
Potocki, Alfred Józef 39
power theory 114–118
psychological violence (bullying) 11

resistance: digital 99; popular examples 2; technology and 71–72; testimony as 80
Rohingya community 136
Russian revolution 34, 43

Saffron Revolution in Myanmar 136
Santa Cruz, Hernán 70
school shootings 12
Sharp, Gene: civil resistance, definition 21; method of nonviolent action 9, 17, 130–134; on oppressor and oppressed 18; *Politics of Nonviolent Action, The* 52; theory of power 115–118
social media: Edroğan/AKP regime 71; HDP's use of 78, 81; mass media agenda 73; political actor's agendas 72, 74; tools 11, 74; use in India 101, 103, 121
structural violence 7–8, 12–16, 18, 22–23

Trump, Donald 8, 72
Turkey: agenda-setting theory 72–74; Amnesty laws 68; Gülenist

movement 67; HDPEnglish issues 74–82; human rights issues 70–71; independence 62; Kurdish movement in 69; Kurdish people struggling, salient topics 74–78; military coups 67; political parties 64–66; situation in Syria 69; situation of Kurds 68; social media 71–78; two-step flow of communication model 72–74

violence: against animals 11–12; direct 11–14, 16, 18; forms of 23; indirect 14

Women's March 137
Women's Suffrage Parade 114
World War I 34

YPG (Peoples Protection Units) 4, 67, 69

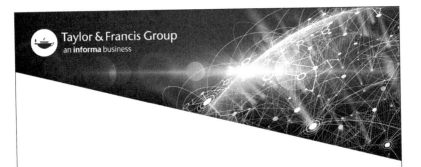